HIDDEN HATE

HIDDEN HATE

HIDDEN HATE

THE RESILIENCE OF XENOPHOBIA

MATHEW CREIGHTON

Columbia University Press   *New York*

Columbia University Press
Publishers Since 1893
New York   Chichester, West Sussex
cup.columbia.edu

Copyright © 2024 Columbia University Press

Library of Congress Cataloging-in-Publication Data

Names: Creighton, Mathew, author.
Title: Hidden hate : the resilience of xenophobia / Mathew Creighton.
Description: 1 Edition. | New York : Columbia University Press, 2023. |
Includes index.
Identifiers: LCCN 2023021837 | ISBN 9780231203166 (hardback) |
ISBN 9780231203173 (trade paperback) | ISBN 9780231554909 (ebook)
Subjects: LCSH: Xenophobia. | Immigrants—Cultural assimilation. |
Emigration and immigration—Government policy. | Toleration—
Political aspects. | Culture conflict.
Classification: LCC HV6250.4.E75 C734 2023 | DDC 305.8—
dc23/eng/20230720
LC record available at https://lccn.loc.gov/2023021837

Printed and bound by CPI Group (UK) Ltd, Croydon, CR0 4YY

Cover design: Noah Arlow

For Atesh

CONTENTS

ACKNOWLEDGMENTS

My first revelation of masked intolerance occurred just as I was shaking off the dust of my PhD years. The ink was still wet on the contract for my first research job, and I recall waiting nervously outside the office of Amaney Jamal during her regularly scheduled office hours. My goal was to convince her to try a survey experiment with me. She provided a commitment and trust that were entirely new to me. She became a keen and consistent coconspirator for my first foray into the world of anonymity, manipulation, and experimentation. Her initial expression of confidence made real much of what I've done since. Although we have moved on to other projects and interests, she remains the intellectual reference for much of my work. As mentioned throughout this book, I also benefited from an exceptional bevy of collaborators. The extensive and diverse fieldwork would not have been successful without Alessandra Bazo Vienrich, Philip Brenner, Natalia Malancu, Frances McGinnity, Peter Schmidt, and Zan Strabac. Finally, there is Hyunjoon Park. There are few bonds like that between a PhD candidate and their supervisor—at least as far as I'm concerned. He taught me kindness, commitment, pragmatism, and collaboration. These are the tools that make something like this possible.

A project like this is also personal. My wife, Yasha Butler, offered a respite from the isolation that writing imposes. I will always appreciate the interest she took in my writing—often not in the content of the prose but in the process of creation. She's an artist and understands better than most what it means to make something out of nothing. My son, Atesh, to whom this book is dedicated, seemed at times to actively conspire to prevent its completion. I would expect nothing else from a child his age, and I rarely found writing to be time better spent. My father, Max Creighton, should have had the chance to read this, and his passing during its writing is something that I will not forgive our recent pandemic. He was a worthy adversary of intolerance, which his life and work reflected. My mother, Susan Jamieson, remains an inspiration and the only person who could plausibly draw a line from my beginning—my true beginning—to what you have before you. My sister, Emily, who is an advocate for the targets of the xenophobia revealed in these pages, is a person whose opinion carries more weight than she realizes. Her opinion is one of insight and strength. I am fortunate to have a family that offers a constellation of people who ground me, distract me, and love me.

HIDDEN HATE

HIDDEN HATE

INTRODUCTION

THE XENOPHOBE AND A MULTILAYERED MODEL OF XENOPHOBIC EXPRESSION

The xenophobe is far from new. However, the xenophobe now navigates an evolving landscape in which the space ceded to open expressions of intolerance is inextricably tied to a contemporary experience of diversity and social norms, which have evolved in parallel. Capturing the attention of scholars, politicians, and the public, emerging evidence reveals the sensitivity of the xenophobe to context—both national and ideological[1]—underlined by notable variation in how newcomers are viewed, supported, and opposed. In effect, the xenophobe, by being present or absent, vocal or silent, can fundamentally shape the landscape of reception for migrants. Again, this is not new, as there is a documented tradition of some people viewing newcomers with suspicion in many, if not all, contexts of reception. What has changed is that the source of this antipathy—the xenophobe—is increasingly strategic. Where we had previously focused only on openly conveyed sentiment, we now understand that the xenophobe is far more nuanced and self-aware. As a result, we—as researchers, bystanders, and participants—need new tools and an evolved perspective to better understand how this changing social landscape shapes the expression of xenophobic intolerance. Despite notable advancements in our understanding of the theoretical and ideological foundation of xenophobia as an increasingly influential idea,[2] little work sees xenophobia as an *act* and, moreover, the xenophobe as an *actor*. This oversight is no longer tenable, which this book does its best to make theoretically and empirically clear.

First, we need to understand how the xenophobe reshapes societies. This issue, at its core, is about humans crossing borders. Alone or in concert, no issue has come to dominate the social and political landscape like migration. Reflected in substantial public interest, the salience of migration in poll data has ascended to the rarefied air of stalwart concerns like health and the economy.[3] It is the tie that binds seemingly disparate but increasingly influential far-right political movements like the Progress Party (FrP; Norway), the Party for Freedom (PVV; the Netherlands), the United Kingdom Independence Party(UKIP), the Northern League or the League (LN; Italy), the True Finns or Finns Party (PS; Finland), the Sweden Democrats (SD; Sweden), Golden Dawn (ANOIX; Greece), Alternative for Germany (AfD), and the Freedom Party of Austria (FPÖ), among others, as well as the post-2016 trajectory of the Republican Party (GOP) in the United States.[4] Few, if any, countries can claim immunity from the pull of antipathy to newcomers, but emergent trends underscore the notable success of a uniformly hardened anti-immigrant stance in otherwise distinct receiving societies. Clearly, opposing newcomers resonates—socially and politically. But with whom? Something is going on that suggests we need to fundamentally rethink how we understand the xenophobe's role and impact.

Second, we need to understand the xenophobe's tactics, which are far more nuanced than evidence, often based on overtly expressed sentiment and public acts or rhetoric, suggests. Defined by time and place, our perception of migration is intertwined

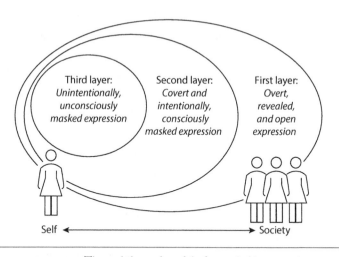

FIGURE 0.1 The multilayered model of xenophobic expression

with economic shocks and political currents, which can change rapidly. These shifts, in turn, shape and reshape the contextual norms governing how and when intolerance can or should be openly expressed. In a sense, society provides the audience for whom the xenophobe performs. As a result, a xenophobic act is best understood as a performance that varies significantly and substantively depending on society's expectations.

How? The primary mechanism is the *stigmatization* of openly articulated xenophobia. As alluded to earlier, the expected condemnation of xenophobic expression results in significant and intentional concealment—the xenophobe's preferred strategy to mitigate social stigma. Although never systematically folded into a general model of the xenophobe, evidence is clear that xenophobic expression is often strategically masked. Addressing and accounting for this emergent strategy of the contemporary xenophobe, this work defines a new, multilayered model of xenophobic expression (figure 0.1). The layers of the model illustrate the pathway by which strategic forms of expression become available to the xenophobe and, moreover, how they are connected to one another.

The first, outer layer captures intolerance that is openly *revealed.* This layer sees xenophobia as an overt stance that, more often than not, can reliably be captured with direct responses to straightforward questions about attitudes toward immigrants or migration.[5] Evidence typically emerges from interviews, surveys, political discourse, and records of public acts. As will become increasingly clear, however, these approaches can limit and occasionally distort our view of the xenophobe. The primary shortcoming of this approach is that we reasonably anticipate situations in which open expressions of intolerance incur a social cost. In these moments, we might not choose to reveal intolerance, preferring to avoid the stigma. That said, much of what we understand about the behavior of the xenophobe is based on this outer layer, which is intuitive given the methodological tool kit historically available to us. However, in an age of migration when societies have adapted to an increasingly diverse demographic reality in which immigrants have played a significant role, we should treat insight gleaned from revealed intolerance with skepticism.

Skepticism does not imply dismissal. At no point do openly expressed and overtly acted-upon forms of xenophobia lack meaning—to the immigrant or the xenophobe. In fact, overt biases often define the day-to-day experience of newcomers and xenophobes alike. As we often experience only what others choose to convey openly, revealed xenophobia is not to be dismissed simply because other options of expression are available. However, it should also not be considered sufficient for an understanding of how and why xenophobia emerges in the first place. Instead, the model introduced here provides a more complete understanding of the xenophobe. It requires a simultaneous acknowledgment of surface-level (i.e., revealed or overt) expressions of intolerance alongside deeper, less easily observed layers. The implications are *substantive* and *interpretive*. Substantively, revealed xenophobia no longer represents a complete or even preferred window into the motives and targets of the xenophobe. Interpretively, insight gleaned from openly revealed sentiment must be read narrowly and, when considered in isolation, assumed to be potentially misleading. Why? Because observing changes in revealed xenophobic expression can conflate the determinants of xenophobia with those of masking. To understand the motives of the xenophobe, we must dig deeper.

The second layer of the model captures what is *not* revealed. It captures xenophobic expression that is *intentionally masked*—an important, albeit often unobserved, source of covert intolerance. Ignoring intentionally masked antipathy can (and often does) paint an overly optimistic picture of the extent to which many contexts of reception are open and tolerant. This sanguine view, particularly given the traction of populist political movements in recent years, can be in stark contrast to outcomes driven by anonymous acts like voting. Understanding and acknowledging that xenophobia can be intentionally masked does not imply that masked expressions of intolerance are more truthful. Unmasking is different from revealing a lie or catching a liar. Instead, as figure 0.1 makes clear, intentionally masked xenophobia is a theoretical *layer* of a broader understanding of intolerant expression. It exists in parallel with other layers and reflects a face of intolerance that is meaningful in some interactions, particularly when anonymity is plausibly maintained. The views expressed at this layer should not be interpreted as reflective of one's true beliefs because expressed views are driven by separate theoretical motives with distinct implications for behavior.

Evidence of strategic and intentional masking has come to light only in recent years. Country-specific cases highlight clear patterns of strategic masking in the United States, the United Kingdom, Ireland, the Netherlands, and Norway.[6] There is more to the story than simply accepting that masking occurs. The level of masking, its cause, and its consequences vary notably across contexts of reception. In other words we can move on from the question of whether masking occurs to the question of why it occurs. Why do some mask intolerance while others reveal it? The answer is found in a potent mechanism and determinant of social interaction: *stigma*.

Our attitudes do not exist in a vacuum. We are members, willingly or unwillingly, of a society. This membership is not without rules. We frequently emphasize or omit details depending on our understanding of how our actions and ideas might be interpreted by others. The result is a strategic and often nuanced presentation that selectively emphasizes or omits certain opinions if we anticipate a positive or negative social consequence. This behavior is particularly relevant when the topic is controversial, which, in the case of migration, is easily anticipated. Expressing opposition to immigration, immigrants, or closely associated out-group characteristics (e.g., religion) overlaps with well-known and oft-stigmatized prejudicial attitudes (e.g., racism, Islamophobia) or historically problematic preferences (e.g., ethnocentrism, nativism). These intersections, which are highly sensitive to context, shape the extent to which social stigma is anticipated. That is, the stigma of revealing xenophobia changes—frequently and with cause. Events like economic austerity or political rhetoric alter the norms governing what is and is not acceptable to reveal. The xenophobe adapts and, on occasion, intentionally misleads. This dynamic back-and-forth between individual attitudes and contextual norms defines the boundary between the covert layer 1, which is revealed, and the covert layer 2, which is intentionally masked.

Consider a case in which more people express opposition to migration relative to an earlier point in time. This situation, defined by a trend of slow change over time, is often observed in contemporary contexts of reception. The interpretation of this trend, assuming no masking occurs, is straightforward. Opposition must be increasing. However, if one considers the possibility of significant and strategic masking, it could just be the case that intolerance simply moved into the open. Understanding the interplay between social stigma and xenophobic expression requires a new perspective on how the xenophobe adapts. On one hand, it is reasonable to look at what people openly say or do as reflective of ideational change. However, acknowledging and accounting for the masked xenophobe allows a more complete picture to emerge. One concrete example is the case of Brexit, which is explored in detail in chapter 4. The successful campaign to take the United Kingdom out of the European Union exploited concerns over refugee migration and speculation about Muslim-majority Turkey entering the European Union, bringing overtly Islamophobic discourse into the political mainstream. Once one accepts that targeted biases are sometimes masked, it becomes clear that an observed increase in concern about Muslim migration among the general public might be reflective of an actual change in opinion or, alternatively, a reduction in the stigma of appearing openly Islamophobic because of the use of the strident political discourse that normalized Muslim migration as a legitimate public target. Failing to distinguish the two invites fundamental misinterpretations of the xenophobe's beliefs and motives.

Intentionality does not determine all forms of masked xenophobia. A third layer of the model captures intolerance that is *unconscious* and by extension *unintentional.* To be clear, the absence of intent does not suggest a reduced impact when compared with sentiment that is revealed (layer 1) or intentionally masked (layer 2). However, the motives are theoretically divergent and imply some level of reduced culpability as well as limited agency. Intention aside, this absence of acknowledgment of intolerance—unintentional or not—can play a substantial role in the perpetuation of biases, which has been noted extensively in the literature on racism. Seemingly race-neutral practices can in some cases contribute to the resilience of social and economic inequities across a variety of domains such as hiring, academic achievement, and law enforcement.[7] Via color-blind, unspoken, unconscious, or unintentional pathways, racial and ethnic hierarchies can be maintained and remain notably resistant to legal and social interventions.[8] This layer of intolerance has proven notoriously difficult to observe because it simultaneously perpetuates and denies prejudice.[9]

The third layer of the multilayered model of xenophobic expression stands apart from the first two layers in that interventions must focus on making what is unknown known—to a society and an individual. Doing so necessitates confronting forms of self-deception using tools that focus on involuntary moments of expression. Instead of directly querying one's opinion (as with revealed expressions) or mitigating social stigma (as with intentional masking) to elicit responses, techniques must often rely on eliciting unconscious associations because unintentional xenophobia endures in individuals who might fully disavow its existence.[10] The general idea is that biases emerge through involuntary behavior reflected in how categories are associated (e.g., positive words and group identities). Although ubiquitous in social psychology and often informative, tests of implicit associations do not offer a foolproof statistical truth serum. However, the impetus for measuring implicit behavior is the view that we compartmentalize our biases, which must be included in any comprehensive and nuanced model of xenophobic expression. The multilayered model of xenophobic expression put forward here is no exception. That said, this work targets the second layer, intentionally masked expression, which has been overlooked while interest in overt expression and unconscious biases have received relatively more attention.

Our task ahead is to untangle the distinct motives and determinants of each layer of the xenophobe, which requires the revelation of context-specific mechanisms that shape and motivate each layer. To avoid an overly abstract argument, carefully selected substantive chapters present concrete examples that leverage specific moments (i.e., the Great Recession, Brexit) and specific contexts (i.e., the United States, the United Kingdom, Ireland, the Netherlands, Norway) to highlight evidence of the overt and covert xenophobe. By clearly linking concrete evidence to a core theoretical model, this book offers a new understanding of the xenophobe as a complex object of inquiry whose beliefs are strategically revealed or hidden depending on context.

PART I: A PRACTICAL AND THEORETICAL PERSPECTIVE ON XENOPHOBIC EXPRESSION

As a starting point, the xenophobe requires definition—both theoretical and practical. For part I of this book, we need a conceptual foundation. The key elements to account for are the reality of the xenophobe as an actor who is subject to a defined context and who seeks expression as a strategic form of self-presentation. The definitional result must be coherent and succinct enough to offer a practical footing upon which a multilayered model can be built. In addition, the definition of the xenophobe must offer the flexibility to capture layered pathways by which xenophobia is expressed. Chapter 1 addresses the diverse yet compartmentalized terminology that plagues our understanding of the xenophobe. The linked but distinct terms *Islamophobe, racist, ethnocentrist,* and *nativist* are examined and common threads exposed. Our goal is a much-needed clarification of an oft-used but poorly coordinated vocabulary of intolerance. A unified definition of the xenophobe emerges that shows the web of connections among targeted terms for intolerances that are rooted in religious, racial, ethnic, and gendered dimensions of xenophobia. At no point is the xenophobe understood to be a fixed entity. Instead, the ability of context and related norms of reference to shape where and when the xenophobe emerges is a key aspect of the model put forward here. To these ends, two key dimensions of xenophobic expression prove crucial: *context* and *strategy.*

First, we establish *context.* To do so requires more than just answers to the questions *when* and *where?* Context defines the relevant norms governing the revelation or masking of intolerance. When establishing context, the key is to avoid overgeneralization, which is of limited value, if not wholly misleading in some cases. Why? Because xenophobic expression is constrained and facilitated by a number of factors such as an anticipation of context-specific social norms, a varied experience of economic and political crises, and divergent or convergent demographic patterns. These considerations, which fundamentally alter the landscape immigrants confront, exist within policy environments that are tied to national or subnational boundaries: social, geographic, and political. Even country-level perspectives should be considered cautiously because subnational social strata (e.g., educational gradients, class categories, urbanicity) can be dominant. However, too finely detailed perspectives can also be problematic. Micro-level observations, although rich and detailed, don't always offer insight at the level at which policy is enacted, nor do they capture group-level norms, which can be derived from broad messages originating in public figures and language-specific media. With an eye toward evidence-driven public policy, the preferred model of xenophobic expression put forward here is pragmatic and applied.

This approach to social theory embraces Merton's middle ground, resisting both the temptation of grand theorizing and overly specific perspectives.[11] Our objective in the pages that follow is to link xenophobia to clearly defined national and subnational borders, which are subject to interpretable and concrete demographic, economic, and political dynamics. Succinctly put, the best articulation of this level of engagement is that of *society*. Through society, we engage with meaningful political borders (real or perceived), consequential social and national identities, defined areas of economic and public policy, systems of collaborative governance, and an interpretable demographic profile. Within this complex but definable landscape, the expression of anti-immigrant sentiment differently targets religious, ethnic, racial, and gendered definitions of newcomers. This variation in targets and the extent to which intolerance can be revealed in turn depends highly on social, economic, and political circumstances. In short, to fully understand how xenophobia is expressed, we must first understand the context—both real and perceived—that shapes the xenophobe's experience.

Once we understand context, *strategy* moves to the fore. To use the analogy of the theater, once the audience is known, our interest turns to the performance. An understanding of xenophobic expression as a tactical instrument is distinct from a perspective that sees antipathy toward immigrants as a straightforward reaction to events (e.g., economic downturns, hardened political rhetoric). A reactive and surface-level view of the xenophobe imagines societies of reception as alternately accepting and rejecting immigration or specific immigrant groups. Such a stance is unlikely; at best, this view provides an incomplete picture of the dynamics at work.

Instead, the xenophobe anticipates context-specific social expectations and reveals intolerance selectively. For the most part, what we see is what the xenophobe intends for us to see. Strategically, it follows that what we *don't* see is perhaps most relevant because these manifestations of the xenophobe emerge in contexts in which antipathy can avoid observation. These contexts are by definition unknown and, without the right tools, might remain unknowable. For example, opposing immigrants of a certain religion might manifest only behind anonymous acts like voting. In stark contrast to existing theories of anti-immigrant sentiment (e.g., threat theory, competition theory, contact theory), a multilayered model of xenophobic expression sees the xenophobe as someone who can present many masks. As such, newfound antipathy might be the result of newly revealed opposition rather than newly emergent intolerance. The difference between the two is significant because the former indicates that the masked xenophobe could make certain types of concealable xenophobia relevant in moments in which overt sentiment would suggest otherwise.

Importantly, the layers of the model presented here are inseparable. Each layer interacts, rather than competes, with the others. As a result, all layers must be considered in concert—as should the strategies underpinning their motives. A xenophobe's tactic of expression is intimately shaped by pivotal events such as the perception of threat—economic or cultural—and elite discourse. The effect on expression is often indirect because the key impact of such events is on social norms, which govern the social stigma one can anticipate when revealing negative or positive attitudes toward particular migrant groups. For example, a single attribute (e.g., belief in Islam) may emerge as an acceptable target in certain moments,[12] whereas another group-level characteristic (e.g., race) remains sheltered from overt antipathy because the social norms in this context differentiate Islamophobia from racism, with the former eliciting less condemnation. The key to understanding these patterns is to acknowledge that the xenophobe does not express a single attitude toward immigrants and therefore is not a fixed entity. Only after the *context* is known can a *strategy* be anticipated.

The first chapter sets the stage, putting into practice a multilayered perspective of xenophobic expression. However, the question of motive remains. Chapter 2 identifies the underlying theoretical mechanism that leads to the revelation of some forms of anti-immigrant sentiment and the masking of others: *social stigma*. The importance of social stigma for situationally defined strategic behavior, although rarely applied to expressions of intolerance, builds from a strong and widely understood intellectual footing. The starting point is the posthumously published work of George Herbert Mead, who recognized an inherently layered organization of human identity.[13] Without this foundational work, a multilayered model of xenophobic expression would be difficult, if not impossible, to put forward. Mead's influence can be traced through seminal work on intergroup relations.[14] But the closest link to the model presented here is found in the work of Erving Goffman, who delineated attributes that can be masked, termed "discreditable." from attributes that cannot, termed "discredited."[15] The initial intention of Goffman's distinction was to understand the symbolic meaning of physical attributes, but the extension to the expression of sentiment is clear.

At its core, chapter 2 reveals xenophobia to be an attribute that is both feasibly discreditable and plausibly the target of negative social stigma—at least in some contexts. The degree of social stigma and, occasionally, its absence is contextually defined. And it follows that the strategy used to intentionally mask xenophobia mitigates stigmatization through the conversion of what might be *discredited* into something that is *discreditable*. In short, masked intolerance is less likely if the expression can be made anonymously. Anonymity is key because it preserves the sentiment but protects the proponent. Chapter 2 introduces a number of feasible methodological solutions, rooted in the multilayered model, that are implemented to simultaneously capture *revealed* (overtly expressed) and *masked* (covertly expressed) xenophobia.

Revealed intolerance is straightforward to measure. The well-honed tools of surveys, interviews, and observation need little introduction. However, masked sentiment is not so easily captured. Introducing a number of unique survey experiments, conducted in multiple receiving contexts (i.e., the United States, the United Kingdom, the Netherlands, Ireland, and Norway), chapter 2 highlights the manipulation of anonymity as a methodological tool. The key comparison is between those who are guaranteed permanent and absolute anonymity and those who express their opinions understanding that they can be known by others—survey takers and the public alike. Chapter 2 provides a scalable, reproducible, and generalizable estimate of the extent to which xenophobic sentiment is masked.

By the conclusion of the first part, we have gained the theoretical and methodological tools necessary to operationalize the multilayered model of xenophobic expression. We now turn to evidence.

PART II: ECONOMIC POPULISM
AND THE POLITICS OF
XENOPHOBIC EXPRESSION

The emergent and contested politics of populism offer unique insight into the layers of xenophobic expression that increasingly define many societies of immigrant reception. Part II unpacks recent political trends in the United States and Europe to reveal how populism, as a social and political movement, resists a singular definition.[16] One perspective frames populism as a reaction to existing (or recently existing) political convention. Populism embodies a rejection of a political establishment and, reflective of a reactionary posture toward older political orientations of the right, is typically characterized ideologically as "new" or "radical."[17] Despite near-incoherent platforms across a variety of country contexts that advocate for distinct (sometimes widely so) economic and political objectives, one issue unites populist insurgencies in the United States and Europe: migration. More specifically, *opposition* to migration. This confrontational and restrictive stance perhaps offers the only unifying ideological and policy orientation and, from the perspective of some, is the key to recent electoral success.[18] But where did this support come from? Is it new, or does it tap into something more stable that remained unobserved? There are answers, but they are not always obvious.

Chapter 3 focuses primarily on the United States and the period of sustained recession following the downturn in the subprime mortgage market in late 2007 and early 2008. In rapid succession, the U.S. Federal Housing Finance Agency placed the backbone of the U.S. mortgage market (i.e., the Federal National Mortgage Association, known as Fannie Mae, and the Federal Home Loan Mortgage Corporation, known as Freddie Mac) under federal conservatorship. Nearly simultaneously, Lehman Brothers, a 158-year-old holding company and investment bank, declared bankruptcy. Although cracks appeared in the mortgage market as early as August 2007, it is September 2008 that has ingrained itself into the public psyche.[19] The results presented in chapter 3, derived from unique survey experiments fielded before and after the financial crisis, show that materialist models of anti-immigrant sentiment, which privilege economic competition (real or perceived) between immigrants and nonimmigrants, are insufficient and in some ways misleading. The materialist perspective often does not accurately predict or describe the motives of an emergent xenophobic public. What appears to have been an uptick in opposition was really a reduced need to mask intolerance, a need that evidence suggests existed to a large extent before the economic downturn. In other words, materialist concerns offer a cover rather than a motive.

The key revelation is that external economic shocks legitimize messages and constituencies that previously necessitated more subtle forms of communication. When social stigma is clearly anticipated, xenophobic expression requires "dog whistling," which relies on subtle messaging to signal a policy position while simultaneously avoiding the stigma of overtly supporting a controversial or condemnable idea. As with a real dog whistle, avoiding stigma requires finding a pitch and wavelength that are interpretable only by the target audience. The financial crisis moved the political conversation into the open by providing a material logic. Such a move avoids the need to reveal biases rooted in sociocultural intolerance (e.g., Islamophobia, racism, ethnocentrism, ethnonationalism), which are more clearly targeted and hence stigmatized forms of intolerance. Chapter 3 shows how and, moreover, why anti-immigrant sentiment became a viable political platform and why xenophobes became an openly courted and undeniably influential constituency in the United States.

To be clear, the move of xenophobic expression into the open does not suggest that xenophobia is new in the United States, nor does it suggest that xenophobia is a stable part of the political conversation. In fact, chapter 3 shows that the overall perception of immigrants in the United States changed little. What did change was the anticipation of stigma, resulting in a significant and substantive shift from masked to revealed intolerance. Opposing immigration did not suddenly become acceptable to those previously in favor (or neutral), which would be the interpretation if only overt sentiment were taken into account. Instead, acknowledging the strategic performance of the xenophobe, which is highly sensitive to context, fundamentally changes our interpretation of the political meaning of the financial crisis. Rather than inventing a concern about immigration or even increasing the popularity of anti-immigrant views, the Great Recession in the United States allowed anti-immigrant sentiment and its political representation (i.e., populism) to move into the mainstream. The relevant layer of the multilayered model of xenophobic expression shifted from the second, which is covert, to the first, which is overt (see figure 0.1). Evidence suggests that messages requiring a certain pitch to avoid detection before the crisis benefited from the destigmatization of xenophobic expression afterward. In short, the dogs were always listening, but the crisis moved anti-immigrant populism into the open, avoiding any need for subterfuge. This context set the stage for an anti-immigrant candidate to become the center of the 2016 presidential campaign and for xenophobes to become an openly defined, influential, and desired constituency.

The United States is far from the only context of reception to be politically (re)shaped by populism and its hardened political discourse directed at immigrants. Chapter 4 shifts to Europe, highlighting Brexit, which is a blanket term for the campaign and vote for and the departure of the United Kingdom from the European Union. As in the case of the United States following the financial crisis, understanding the link between populism and xenophobic expression reveals a new of view of the meaning of Brexit for UK society. In the case of Brexit, the campaigns consisted of two competing messages defined in large part by the issue of borders and by extension movement across them. Messages in favor of leaving the European Union coupled materialist arguments—notably service provision tied to the funding of health care—with anxiety about the border—particularly in regard to newcomers from Muslim-majority countries. Support for the "remain" side countered these arguments by pointing out that targeted anti-immigrant rhetoric activated and benefited from racial and religious intolerance. The two campaigns simultaneously stigmatized and legitimized the expression of xenophobia.[20] In the end, both campaigns enjoyed notable success.

Resisting a simplistic interpretation of Brexit, this chapter explains why some political rhetoric reveals antipathy toward some migrant groups but obscures intolerance toward others. Leveraging data from two unique survey experiments collected before and after the Brexit campaigns, chapter 4 shows that the expression of attitudes toward migrants to the United Kingdom was highly sensitive to how the issue was framed (e.g., national origin, religion, race). The Brexit campaigns unsettled the norms governing the expression of intolerance, and the xenophobe adapted to navigate this changed normative landscape. New patterns of social stigma emerged, determined by both campaigns, which increased the reluctance of some to express antipathy. Others, defined by political stripe and social status, felt emboldened in the post-Brexit landscape to express attitudes they had previously masked. Some immigrant groups, notably Muslims, were disproportionately affected by the change in social climate, whereas other groups experienced little difference. The case of the United Kingdom further anchors our understanding of expressed xenophobia as a strategic and, evidence suggests, rapid reaction to context. The xenophobe must navigate a climate of competing messages and seek strategies that reflect changing expectations about which types of expression will elicit—and which types will avoid—social stigma.

PART III: RACE, RELIGION, AND REFUGEES: THE EXPRESSION OF TARGETED INTOLERANCE

Shifting from examples that explore material and sociopolitical contexts, part III asks a somewhat different question: How does the xenophobe navigate race, religion, and morality? Chapter 5 considers race. Recent influential and insightful work on racial attitudes in the United States highlights the importance and implications of color-blind racism—a term that defines the simultaneous practice and denial of racial prejudice.[21] Although the denial of intolerance is often portrayed as unconscious, indicating a degree of self-deception, it is also plausible that such denial reflects intentionality. Leveraging evidence of color-blind racism, chapter 5 shows how framing migration with a racial lens shapes the extent to which antipathy is revealed in multiple European contexts. Importantly, the role of race is rarely observable when only overt, surface-level sentiment is taken into account.

The key insight is this: when migrant groups are framed by race, a significant part of the ambivalence and, in some cases, support for migration is an aberration. When xenophobes are provided permanent and absolute anonymity, public sentiment is characterized by a notably higher level of antipathy. This pattern proves that some targeted biases are illusory or, more specifically, limited to a single layer of xenophobic expression. As a result, observed differences in revealed attitudes toward immigrant groups defined by race relative those defined by something else (e.g., religion, country of origin) disappear when intentionally masked sentiment is accounted for. This evidence builds an empirical bridge between a multilayered model of xenophobic expression and the large literature on the perpetuation of racial intolerance. Both perspectives agree that prejudicial attitudes persist among those who actively deny their existence, but the work presented here provides new insight into a covert layer of racially motivated xenophobia that is strategically and intentionally masked. In other words, in multiple contexts, the xenophobe harbors racial intolerance but is savvy and strategic. In the absence of anonymity, race-neutral narratives are performed first to mitigate anticipated stigmatization. Without a multilayered model, revealed anti-immigrant sentiment might be taken to be sufficient to understand the motives of xenophobic expression. But this view would leave many with the false impression that race is of little consequence in contexts in which it is, instead, significantly masked.

Chapter 6 shifts from race to religion, focusing on Islamophobia in the United States and Europe. Although migration from Muslim-majority countries has emerged as a recent flash point in some contexts of reception, the use of religion as a marker to delineate the autochthonous from the newcomer is far from original.[22] Xenophobic expression easily anticipates historically rooted norms that govern how intolerance toward specific religious groups will be perceived and in some cases stigmatized. Three contexts offer unique insight into how this plays out: the United States, the United Kingdom, and Norway. The results highlight, once again, how wrong we can be when we ignore masked xenophobia.

Despite notable differences in context and strategy, a broad—and startling—pattern emerges. In the contexts examined, Muslim immigrants are openly targeted despite little difference in attitudes under conditions of anonymity. In short, anti-immigrant views, including opposition to migrant groups defined by religions other than Islam, are selectively and strategically expressed. Being an Islamophobe does not require such strategic masking. Muslim immigrants confront notably overt opposition, whereas other immigrant religious communities experience a more nuanced and hesitant form of intolerance. One implication of this context is that Islamophobia—as a distinct form of xenophobia—is better understood as a form of intolerance that is not subject to significant social stigma. It resides in the outermost layer (i.e., covert expression), whereas other forms of antipathy that target more socioculturally proximate religions or immigrant characteristics emerge only when deeper layers of expression are bought into focus (see figure 0.1).

Refugee migration, particularly from Muslim-majority countries, emerged as a salient point of contention in post-2015 contexts of reception in Europe and more broadly. The perception of large-scale movement from the Global South via Mediterranean countries created tension in some receiving contexts between a moral imperative to provide aid and anxieties rooted in national or sociocultural identity. Chapter 7 reveals how this tension shapes the expression of intolerance in Norway, which provides asylum to many Muslim newcomers, particularly relative to the national population. To understand how refugees are distinguished from other types of migrants, several frames offer a dynamic perspective on the highly politicized, morally problematic, and rapid evolution of anti-refugee sentiment. Few have explored this type of intolerance in detail, in part because of the substantial degree of masking one might expect. Opposing those facing persecution is plausibly more controversial relative to arguments rooted in material or even sociocultural logics.

Evidence reveals a troubling pattern. Refugee migration is one of the most sympathetic forms of migration and is rooted in a moral imperative; however, refugees are increasingly experiencing a similar level of hostility to that experienced by nonrefugee immigrant groups—even in historically welcoming contexts like Norway. Results show that the xenophobe systematically masks refugee opposition, which indicates that antipathy toward asylum-based migration is morally and socially problematic even to those who find antipathy appealing. This context has implications for anonymous behavior, suggesting the clear utility of (even indirectly) activating refugee-based opposition as a means of generating a political constituency or support for a related social movement.

This book asks us to fundamentally rethink our understanding of the xenophobe. When the xenophobe is treated as an independent object deserving of study, a multilayered model emerges that provides a clear sense of how xenophobia, as an act, is performed. Once we account for context and strategy, surface-level observations of intolerance, when considered independently, prove to be of limited value. Instead, observing how, and when, the xenophobe expresses intolerance is an invitation to be an audience member in a potentially carefully choreographic performance. Although it is useful to know how those who hold antipathy toward newcomers seek to present themselves, covert expression is only one layer of expression, and on occasion not a particularly informative one at that.

This book's first part argues forcefully—theoretically and methodologically—for an approach that considers revealed and masked layers of xenophobia in parallel. If we are truly to understand the role of xenophobia in shaping societies of reception, intentionally and unintentionally hidden dimensions of intolerance prove inimitably insightful. It is one thing to make an abstract and theoretical case for a multilayered model of xenophobic expression. Providing evidence is another matter altogether. Parts II and III operationalize the theoretical and methodological solutions introduced in the first. By way of unique and targeted survey experiments that use anonymity to mitigate the role of social stigma, a clear and complete picture of the xenophobe is able to emerge. Attitudes that, under normal observation, remain unknown and unknowable, are placed in stark relief. The results unmask the role of context (e.g., economic crisis, political competition) and specific attributes of targeted immigrant groups (e.g., race, ethnicity, religion) in determining what is revealed and, moreover, what is strategically withheld.

Evidence shows that the (re)emergence of overt anti-immigrant sentiment in response to economic crises or strident political discourse obscures a substantial and often stable well of xenophobia. Society changes, as do the norms governing xenophobic expression—that much is clear—but these shifts can reflect an increased acceptance of intolerance rather than an increase in intolerance itself. This work, combining a theoretical multilayered model with unique empirical evidence in multiple country contexts, challenges the narrative that emergent patterns of antipathy toward migration and migrants reflect a fundamental change in previously receptive societies. Instead, this book asks that we critically engage with the multilayered performance of the xenophobe. Only when the xenophobe's many masks are taken into account can we truly confront the roots of intolerance.

I

A PRACTICAL AND THEORETICAL PERSPECTIVE ON XENOPHOBIC EXPRESSION

1

WHO IS THE XENOPHOBE?

ISLAMOPHOBES, RACISTS, ETHNOCENTRISTS, AND NATIVISTS

Who is the xenophobe? A predictable starting point is the Greek origin of the word, which couples the concepts of the stranger (*xénos*) and fear (*phóbos*). This appears to be a straightforward definition, but it's an illusion. For one, who is the fearful? Moreover, who is to be feared? The answers to both questions are core to the concept, but both have changed over time and place. From the outset, to define the xenophobe requires us to define the stranger. Georg Simmel, a prominent sociologist at the turn of the last century, sought to frame the stranger in a way that could transcend place and time—as a sort of abstract other.[1]

This grand-theory approach has drawbacks, which will be made clear in the many contexts explored in this book that resist a static definition of the xenophobe. But Simmel does offer a foundational perspective that sees the stranger as a social actor who navigates a social context. This view delineates groups with which one identifies (in-groups) from those with which one does not (out-groups). Less emphasized by Simmel is the importance of context, variation in which shapes whom the xenophobe fears and helps illuminate overlapping options in group membership. The stranger might live nearby, share a passport, and even share the same moment in time, but Simmel (and others[2]) point out that what defines a stranger is in the eyes of the beholder: a socially constructed identity that can surmount any national, legal, or political definition.

This perspective allows for some flexibility in that identity; while often durable and resilient, it is not innate and requires social context to become concrete—even temporarily. It is constructed by circumstances and socialization. Even when legal and jurisdictional boundaries are overcome, the label "stranger" can remain stubbornly tied to one's social group, which is a persistent marker of difference and target of the xenophobe. There is a sociological tradition intent on determining the attributes of the xenophobe's target. But evidence, including that presented here, questions the value of broad theoretical traditions that accept the premise that the stranger is fixed within a defined geography. Depending on the context and interaction, the model of xenophobic expression presented here puts forward a perspective and supports evidence that allows for the xenophobe to emerge in distinct pathways of expression—some overt and others masked.

Despite receiving more than a century of attention in social science, the xenophobe has largely avoided any semblance of definitional consensus. But not for lack of trying. What has emerged instead is an expanding menu of terms that focus to differing degrees on specific *out-groups* (the feared) and *in-groups* (the fearful). However, this approach can overlook commonalities in how intolerance emerges at the group level. Specific attributes of the in-group or out-group are privileged over the context within which they are targeted. For example, an out-group focus on religion might highlight the Islamophobe, whereas nationalism among an in-group is captured by highlighting the nativist. When the race of the in-group is the focus, the ethnocentrist might stand in for the xenophobe. For the same divide, when the out-group is the focus, the racist comes to the fore. To be clear, racism is not—nor could it be—a simple subtype of a general concept like xenophobia. The historical, legal, and social origins and implications, as in Islamophobia's link to Orientalism,[3] are relevant and, for some questions, overshadow any need to engage with a layered view of the xenophobe. The point in addressing commonalities is that the xenophobe can use race, like religion, as a bright line delineating who is (and is not) a member of the preferred out-group.[4] Racism—in its interactive and structural form—has reach far beyond the terrain of the xenophobe. As such, the racist and the xenophobe overlap only in a limited, situationally determined way. That said, these distinct but overlapping categories closely track the salience of group-level attributes (e.g., religion) in defining in-groups and out-groups, which can, and often does, change over time and across social and political boundaries.

To offer a clearer example, let's consider the case of the Islamophobe. In understanding migrant contexts of reception, Islamophobes have only relatively recently become of sociological interest, eliciting independent study and distinct theoretical consideration.[5] Work in this vein underscores the intersection of twenty-first-century geopolitical concerns, changing patterns of migration, and the politics of race and religion. In other, more targeted work, political issues like referenda,[6] asylum,[7] electoral politics,[8] religious affiliation,[9] and empire[10] have been shown to be critical for understanding why Islamophobia is an increasingly salient form of intolerance—and why the Islamophobe has found a way into the mainstream. There has been an intense shift in focus toward newcomers from contexts in which Islam is dominant. This foregrounding of Islamophobic sentiment, expressed in public opinion and political choice, reflects a reconfiguration of the norms dictating how and to what extent antipathy can overtly target Muslim newcomers. The Islamophobe is well worth considering as an independent dimension of societal intolerance, but understanding its link to a more general construct—the xenophobe—is also important. Again, context matters. The stranger, defined here as Muslim, and the extent to which this stranger "deserves" antipathy in the mind of the xenophobe are defined by a place and time. Neither the target nor the xenophobe is static: the mechanisms of intolerance are contextually determined.

The ethnocentrist privileges similarity, often as defined by ethnicity or race, and emerged as a category of intolerance early in academic efforts to understand antipathy toward strangers.[11] Depending on the strength of the link made among ethnicity, race, and national identity, ethnocentrists and nativists—another relative of the xenophobe—often conceptually overlap and thus can be considered in concert. Ethnocentrists, in particular, express preference for others who fit an in-group ethnic category that need not be restricted by national boundaries and that can embrace abstract groups linked only loosely to geography or time (e.g., Westerners). Nativism privileges a claim to territory—geographic and cultural—based on prior residence, which is often classified as a birthright, and the in-group identity that such a territorial claim affords.[12] The nativist and the ethnocentrist are tied to frequently changing contextual factors like near-arbitrary periods of colonial expansion and contraction and forms of imposed demographic change (e.g., purges, genocide, pogroms, refugee migration). Ethnic and racial homogeneity are rarely, if ever, applicable to a specific geography over time. The tie that binds ethnocentrists is the expression of a preference based on similarity, regardless of how situationally specific that similarity might be. Co-ethnics and co-nationals, captured by archaic terms like *autochthonous*, frame attitudes toward strangers via an exclusionary preference for a hypothetical and averaged self—an in-group bias. Antipathy toward others, albeit predictable, is born from a perception—real or imagined—that although others might live nearby, they do not share an ethnic, racial, or national attribute. In short, the nativist and the ethnocentrist—in contrast to the Islamophobe—embody the inward-looking dimension of the xenophobe.

Despite this fractured landscape, all xenophobes are united by two key elements: *context* and *strategy*. Understanding these concepts allows for pragmatic flexibility and avoids the temptation of a singular, static, and overly generalized theoretical definition. As the xenophobe is a manifestation of two changing mechanisms, it is more enlightening to understand the when, the where, and the why of the xenophobe. Rather than treating the xenophobe as a permanent, free-floating embodiment of intolerance that is set in opposition to an abstract stranger, the approach taken here privileges the contextual determinants of social identity and finds common threads between various manifestations of the xenophobe. Moreover, an understanding of the relevant context helps to reveal the expressive strategy adopted by the xenophobe. Quibbling about whether the Islamophobe and the ethnocentrist are distinct or similar, for example, can be avoided. Instead, for those domains of intolerance, the objective is to understand why the xenophobe targets certain religions in some moments and racial homogeneity in others. To do this, understanding context comes first.

CONTEXT

To establish *context* requires more than just answers to the questions *when* and *where*? Context also captures the societal rules that govern how and when intolerance is expressed. Anticipating these context-specific social norms shapes how the expression of xenophobia is likely to be interpreted and, by extension, the cost–benefit ratio of such expression. These considerations, which fundamentally alter the reception that migrants encounter, do not exist in a vacuum. Instead, they are intimately tied to a policy environment, an economic situation, and national or subnational boundaries: social, geographic, and political. Scale matters, and the xenophobe can be situated within numerous and overlapping reference contexts. Country-level perspectives should be considered cautiously because subnational social strata (e.g., educational gradients, class categories, urbanicity) may be more relevant and, in many instances, dominant. However, too fine a detail is also problematic. Micro-level observations, although rich and detailed, don't always offer insight at the level at which policy is enacted. Nor do they capture well group-level norms derived from broader messages originating from public figures and language-specific media. With an eye toward evidence-driven public policy, the model of xenophobic expression outlined here is pragmatic and applied.

The relevant level of engagement is that of *society*. Through society, we engage with meaningful political borders (real or perceived), consequential social and national identities, defined areas of economic and public policy, systems of collaborative governance, and an interpretable demographic profile. Within this complex but definable landscape, the expression of anti-immigrant sentiment differently targets religious, ethnic, racial, and gendered definitions of newcomers. This variation in targets and the extent to which intolerance can be revealed in turn depends highly on the context within which intolerance is expressed. Thus, to fully understand how xenophobia is expressed, we must first understand the societal context—both real and perceived—that shapes the xenophobe's experience.

Let's consider the case of the recent referendum to decide the fate of the United Kingdom's membership in the European Union. A dominant focus of both the pro- and anti-Brexit campaigns was the issue of migrants and migration, particularly from Muslim-majority countries, although newcomers from other EU countries were never absent from the debate.[13] In fact, control of national borders—broadly defined—was a consistent refrain of those in favor of leaving the European Union. The stranger was clearly the target, but the specific circumstances of the relationship between the United Kingdom and the European Union provide the contextual factors necessary to define the xenophobe. First, a recent experience of refugee migration to some parts of the European Union. Second, a strident political movement that focused on national borders. This temporally specific mix created a definable context in which antipathy toward immigrants found its voice. As the issue of Muslim immigration was foregrounded, the Islamophobe and the nativist emerged as salient—and complementary—manifestations of xenophobia.

Contentious politics aside (e.g., Brexit), material concerns are thought to define our attitudes toward others like little else. Shaped by an individual-level perception of competition[14] for work or wages or a creeping meso-level uncertainty born of financial precarity,[15] the materialist perspective is seen as a key determinant of xenophobia. Put simply, the economy makes us intolerant—at least when things are not going well. Certainly, recent events seem to support this perspective. The financial crisis that began in late 2007 saw many economies badly battered, and these same contexts were often recent net recipients of newcomers via labor migration or family reunification. The economic downturn quickly began to bite, and *austerity* became a household word. Economies contracted, unemployment increased, and wages stagnated. Even as immigration flows declined—even reversing temporarily in some contexts—economic nationalism and a perception that migrants were unnecessary and unwelcome competition was seen as a mainstream rationale. No religious, national, or ethnic target was required to frame the sentiment because the emergent xenophobic reaction hewed closely to a material logic. What seems to have been questioned less in postcrisis contexts is the extent to which newly vocal opposition was truly new. Instead, in austerity-hit destination contexts, xenophobes confronted a changed landscape in which economic concerns dominated. Rather than suddenly becoming relevant, perceived threats to employment and wages provided a less stigmatized way to express intolerance. Just as Brexit created a context that put a face on the fearful and the feared, austerity provided narratives of economic necessity. These are the contexts within which the xenophobe operates. A general material concern born from an economic meltdown facilitated a more general anti-immigrant posture relative to the narrower religious, geopolitical, and historical contexts of relations between the United Kingdom and the European Union.

Whereas context offers pathways through which antipathy toward newcomers can pass, how this xenophobic sentiment is expressed is best understood as a strategic choice. Once context is known—and only once it is known—*strategy* comes to the fore. Rather than *when* and *where*, strategy explains *why*. It is one thing to underline moments when targeted opposition to certain types of migration (e.g., Muslim refugees, Central American families, EU labor migrants) emerges as uniquely salient. It is quite another to understand why some do (and others do not) take advantage of these moments to strategically express antipathy. The key theoretical step is to understand the concrete role of social context— society—in opening the doors through which the xenophobe can strategically pass. This understanding differs from one in which the xenophobe is seen to be "caused" by a change in material, social, or political circumstances. Instead, this theoretical perspective addresses how the xenophobe emerges and interacts with others. The mechanism of interest is that which determines why some types of intolerance emerge and why some types remain hidden—even from the individual. This brings us to the second element that unites xenophobes: *strategy*.

STRATEGY

Once the audience is known, our interest turns to the performance. The audience and performance, in this case, are analogous to context and strategy. Strategy focuses on the masking of xenophobic sentiment as an intentional act. Moreover, viewing the xenophobe as a tactician is distinct from a perspective that sees antipathy toward immigrants as a simple reaction to events (e.g., economic downturns, hardened political rhetoric). A reactive and surface-level view of the xenophobe imagines societies of reception as alternately accepting and rejecting immigration or specific immigrant groups. This perspective provides at best an incomplete picture of the dynamics at work. A better approach considers the selective presentation of intolerance and strategic masking as a viable, often desirable, social strategy.

The xenophobe anticipates context-specific social expectations and selectively reveals intolerance accordingly. What we see is what is intended to be shown. Strategically, it follows that what we *don't* see is perhaps most relevant, defining domains in which antipathy can avoid observation. For example, openly opposing immigrants of a certain religion might find traction only by way of anonymous acts like voting. In contrast to existing theories of anti-immigrant sentiment (e.g., threat theory, competition theory, contact theory), a multilayered model of xenophobic expression sees the xenophobe as someone who wears many masks. In this model, newfound antipathy might be the result of newly revealed opposition rather than newly emergent intolerance.

However, the layers of the model are inseparable. Each layer complements, rather than competes with, the others, and each must be considered in concert with the others—as should the strategies underpinning what is said and, more to the point, what remains unsaid. Strategies emerge such that the open expression of certain types of antipathy is seen as strategically more (or less) advantageous depending on a definable social context. The effect is often indirect. For example, a particular immigrant characteristic (e.g., belief in Islam) may emerge as an acceptable target in certain moments[16] whereas another group-level characteristic (e.g., race) remains sheltered from overt antipathy because the societal context differentiates Islamophobia from racism, with the former eliciting less condemnation.[17] The key to understanding these patterns is to acknowledge that the xenophobe does not express a single attitude but instead first considers context and then strategically presents distinct masks that best reflect anticipated social consequences. Again, only once *context* is known does a *strategy* emerge (figure 1.1).

The strategy that the xenophobe deploys to navigate a given context is dictated by social pressure to reveal and conceal certain types of expression. To understand this mechanism requires the introduction of a key concept: *stigma*. Stigma is a well-known determinant of social interaction, and its role is not limited to the xenophobe. It provides the primary motivation to mask intolerance and as such is a key dimension of the multilayered model of xenophobic expression. Chapter 2 explores the implications of stigma in greater detail, but the key element to highlight

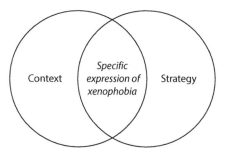

FIGURE 1.1 The relationship between context and strategy for the xenophobe

at this stage is its role in (re)shaping the rules governing what view are and are not acceptable to express. For example, when economic concerns are at the fore, antipathy toward newcomers can be expressed with limited stigma so long as the rationale is economic. This context differs from one in which material concerns are considered to *create* the xenophobe. In the context of an economic downturn, the xenophobe borrows a narrative of competition for employment or wages to convey preexisting intolerances via strategically advantageous layers of expression. Why? Because the material context provides the opportunity, and the evasion of social stigma dictates the strategy.

Focusing on the materialist motives for intolerance is simply illustrative. It provides an accessible example of the xenophobe because competition and threat theories of anti-immigrant sentiment are ubiquitous in the academic literature and in society more broadly, as reflected in strident political rhetoric. That said, it would have been just as easy to highlight the Islamophobe. The 2015 influx of refugees, who were often framed by their Muslim-majority contexts of origin, at the European Union's southern border resulted in a context in which the stranger was seen as Muslim. The issue was not about scale, as refugee flows were a comparatively small component of the migrant populaton in most contexts of reception at their moment of arrival. Demographically, the European Union is composed of much larger populations from previous migration flows—and from countries of origin within the European Union. It was the newness and perceived intensity of the refugee flow, fueled by violence and material deprivation, that resulted in a greater openness to targeted antipathy toward Muslim migration more broadly, rooted in narratives of sociocultural incompatibility. This acceptance of antipathy toward newcomers framed as Muslim greatly reduced the stigma the xenophobe might have anticipated—certainly relative to other out-groups such as labor migrants and migrants defined by race or class. The documented uptick in the expression of anti-Muslim xenophobia, explored in greater detail in chapters 6 and 7, is better understood as strategic opportunism. The antipathy was already there and demonstrably shared with migrants framed in other ways, but the strategy of expression reacted to a shift in anticipated social stigma such that Islamophobic narratives were plausibly interpreted as eliciting less social stigmatization.

My goal in this chapter is to describe how context and strategy, as defined by stigma, work together to shape the types of expression that constitute the distinct layers of the multilayered model of xenophobic expression. It is not to explain the emergence of the xenophobe as a new entity. Frankly, in the contexts explored in this book, the xenophobe is unlikely to be new. Instead, the model offers insight into xenophobic expression by those who need not be newly accepting of intolerance. The creation of the xenophobe is likely linked to forms of socialization very early in the life course and as such is not the focus here. This book offers a perspective that rejects overgeneralized definitions in favor of a midrange framework that explains when and under what circumstances the xenophobe finds a voice.

A CONCISE DEFINITION OF THE XENOPHOBE: ACTORS, ACTS, AND AUDIENCES

For those in search of an analogy, the best one for the xenophobe is that of an actor. The context is the stage. The strategy is the act. The expected reaction of the audience is the anticipated stigma that shapes how the performance unfolds. This dramaturgical perspective is not new and, to be honest, is somewhat overused in sociology. "All the world's a stage" is professed so often and applied in so many circumstances that it risks becoming meaningless. However, in the case of the xenophobe, the analogy of the stage remains useful. It offers a clear way to visualize how multilayered xenophobic expression is practiced.

The first layer we confront is that of openly expressed intolerance (see figure 0.1 in the introduction). This layer captures surface-level antipathy. The xenophobe, as the actor, navigates a context and interaction without inhibition—either social or legal. The presence or absence of stigma depends on the context, which shapes the strategy of expression and therefore the target of antipathy. As discussed, media attention or political opportunity can reduce the stigma of targeted intolerance. For instance, the pro-Brexit campaign mainstreamed Islamophobia,[18] but race-based forms of opposition remained unexpressed. This case highlights the fact that even when the xenophobe finds some open outlets of expression, stigma continues to be anticipated for other forms of intolerance, which therefore remain unexpressed—at least overtly.

This brings us to the second layer, defined by consciously masked antipathy. This layer, which is the key contribution of the model and receives the bulk of the empirical attention in this book, is less frequently acknowledged. I suggest—and offer evidence throughout this book to support—the notion that the strategically masked xenophobe is a repository of a nontrivial amount of intolerance in diverse contemporary Western contexts. These contexts have well-articulated legal and societal limits on the expression of targeted intolerance that provide the xenophobe with an easily anticipated, clear rationale to pursue covert expression. In these contexts, rather than accepting the premise that observed increases in targeted opposition (e.g., Islamophobia during or following a political campaign) reflect a new intolerance, we consider that the conscious masking of antipathy indicates a well of intolerance intentionally hidden from public display. This stance differs substantially from an interpretation that considers a decline in overt xenophobia to indicate a decline in the prevalence of xenophobes in the same context. Trends in observed xenophobic sentiment capture a strategic and opportunistic unmasking rather than the emergence of something new. One can think of the xenophobe as a dynamic actor who adapts their performance in anticipation of the reaction of the audience. This selective unmasking occurs as a result of the interplay of context and strategy, which are the two crucial factors that shape the overt and covert xenophobe.

Intentionally masked intolerance is by definition frequently overlooked. That is the goal after all. This omission shows the reality of societies that are increasingly self-aware of the social stigmatization and consequences, often legal, of targeted biases. In recent memory, institutions as varied as the British royal family[19] and the U.S. Federal Housing Administration[20] openly discriminated in hiring and the provision of service based on race. In recent years, fortunately, the public space available to overt expressions of racism, offered here as a specific manifestation of xenophobia, has shrunk. However, the second layer of the multilayered model of xenophobic expression, defined by an intentional and strategic avoidance of public revelation, provides a resilient repository of prejudice that is somewhat insulated from the social stigmatization of intolerance. This masking does not mean that social stigma is irrelevant. Quite the contrary. Social stigma is the key determinant of the extent to which xenophobes seek covert outlets of expression. In other words, the prevalence of xenophobes in a given context could remain stable while the expression of xenophobic sentiment shifts from overt to covert. In this transition, the xenophobe is an active participant with strategic objectives for a desired outcome.

The third layer of the model captures unconscious forms of xenophobia. If the first layer captures the access the xenophobe has to the public square, the second and third layers are aspects of the xenophobe's hidden world. The second layer is intentional and as such is of greater moral consequence than the third layer because it is involves agency on the part of the intolerant. The third layer emerges from a form of self-deception. As has been pointed out,[21] unconscious forms of intolerance can be, and often are, actively denied. The source of unconscious biases is contested, as are the methods available to mitigate them. The distinguishing feature of the third layer is the imperviousness of unconscious forms of xenophobia to the anticipation of social stigma. In essence, one cannot easily avoid what one is unaware of. As a result, the third layer of xenophobic expression is largely immune to the limiting role of social stigma, which fundamentally shapes the first and second layers.

Now that we have an understanding of the key elements that shape the xenophobe, we can proceed with a clearer understanding of the multilayered model of xenophobic expression, which provides a complete picture of the various and overlapping ways that intolerance is expressed. The theoretical differences and commonalities among the three layers will be explored in detail in the chapters that follow. At this point, however, the key detail to take away is an understanding that the xenophobe is a *contextually determined strategic actor*. This insight is particular to the first two layers of the model, which require intentionality and as such afford room for strategic acts. The motives that shape the emergence, prevalence, and persistence of the xenophobe can be anticipated (and mitigated) only once context and strategy are clearly understood. The model provides a more nuanced view of the xenophobe than those that rely only on overt expression, and to operationalize it requires a unique observational tool kit. In addition, the model underscores the futility of conceptualizing the xenophobe as a static and permanent actor. Xenophobia is not an innate characteristic, and it can exist in multiple layers simultaneously. In other words, xenophobia can be a relevant— and even dominant—characteristic of a person in some contexts, but it can be absent in others.

Observing the first layer is straightforward. The open xenophobe makes no effort to conceal their beliefs and is therefore easy enough to detect. Any standard survey or direct interaction, regardless of the instigator, would suffice. Unfortunately, overt intolerance is often mistaken for an accurate measure of the prevalence of xenophobic expression—full stop. Although the first layer is informative, the second and third layers (consciously and unconsciously masked xenophobia, respectively) have become plausibly important, if not dominant, in many contexts of reception in which tolerance is a referenceable norm. This erodes the viability of viewing overt expression as a generalizable proxy for the contemporary xenophobe. To access the second and third layers of the model, new tools are required—and are available. Unique to this work is a concerted effort to gain access to covert layers of intolerance.

The second layer, covert expression, is characterized by intentional masking. If the xenophobe is successful, this layer should remain undetected and potentially undetectable. As mentioned, the stigmatization of intolerance encourages intentional masking as a strategy to avoid stigma. For the same reason, the alleviation of social stigma can drive a shift from covert to overt expression—so long as the xenophobe is aware of their biases (i.e., their masking is intentional and strategic). The approach taken in the data collection for this book involved providing *permanent and absolute anonymity*. Rather than a promise that a participant's identity will be decoupled from the measure of (in)tolerance, which requires an implausibly high level of trust between the participant and the researcher, this work considers only techniques that avoid any possibility of linking a statement of intolerance with an individual respondent. To operationalize the multilayered model of xenophobic expression, social stigma must be anticipated and mitigated. If not, the observed prevalence and patterning of xenophobic expression over time will be misleading or, at best, limited to the first layer of the model. Anonymity is crucial because it plausibly captures intentionally masked intolerance by offering a context in which sentiment can be expressed in the absence of social stigma. That said, anonymity offers little insight into expressions of the third layer, which are unconscious and somewhat immune to the stigmatization. Assessing the third layer requires a different tool kit because the goal is to focus on cognition and automatic responses rather than expression as shaped by context and strategy. Efforts to understand unconscious or unintentionally masked intolerance benefit less from the provision of anonymity and as such remain outside the scope of the techniques used in the research for much of this book.

TRUTH, DECEPTION, AND
THE MULTILAYERED XENOPHOBE

Observing the masked xenophobe does not provide a window into the truth in some fundamental sense. We must resist the tendency in academia and in everyday life to interpret masked xenophobia, both conscious and unconscious, in absolute terms. In other words, the multilayered model of xenophobic expression, in which the layers exist in parallel, might be interpreted such that the deeper layers are more "true." This is not the case. Penetrating concealment, whether intentional or not, does not uncover a hidden truth in any pure sense. Rather, it is more useful to consider each layer of deception as being "true" only in a certain context and when reflective of a specific strategy, while maintaining an awareness that both context and strategy can and do change. Deception as a tool to mask xenophobia can meaningfully limit the extent to which the xenophobe can find expression in some public domains (e.g., political campaigns, advertising, job postings, admissions criteria). That does not mean that covert expression is where the "real" xenophobe resides.

Just as anonymous comments on the internet are not necessarily more honest expressions of a person's beliefs than those with names attached, anonymous expressions of xenophobia are not necessarily expressions of what one feels in their heart of hearts. For example, the rhetoric deployed on the campaign trail might be constrained by the anticipation of social stigma. However, voting, often an anonymous act, remains a viable outlet for the xenophobe. You might see masked appeals (known as "dog whistling") that signal the possibility of xenophobes as a potential constituency. Such appeals can create and reinforce intolerance in some domains, but they also illuminate the line across which the xenophobe might anticipate stigmatization. As a result, intolerance can persist in terms of experience and expression so long as social stigma can be avoided. This does not mean that the covert xenophobe is the "true" xenophobe in some absolute sense. In the absence of covert forms of expression, overt expressions of intolerance might remain the most impactful—and as such the "truest" to those targeted by intolerance.

Unconscious forms of xenophobic expression, like the intentional masking that constitutes the second layer of the model, may influence some types of interactions but be wholly absent from others. For example, unconscious biases are not necessarily encouraged by those who hold them. Doing so would be a contradiction, given that those biases remain masked even from the individuals who hold them. In contrast to intentional deception, which is consciously shaped, unconscious biases operate outside the realm of volition and are thus a pernicious form of self-deception. Although the evidence is mixed as to whether we can be trained to mitigate our latent biases,[22] simply applying the brakes to one's ability to operate as an unfettered xenophobe is plausible. Composition balance in contexts such as hiring panels, editorial boards, and awards committees are potential interventions that operate under the idea that unconscious forms of intolerance do not reflect a permanent reality but can be mitigated by acknowledging their presence and identifying moments in which these biases might influence substantive outcomes. Given that intolerance is both consciously and unconsciously masked, the multilayered xenophobe is defined by occasionally divergent types of expression. Each is true in certain interactions and less so in others.

To understand the xenophobe requires some acceptance on our part that truth is a relative concept. The xenophobe is less a single entity than a manifestation of specific, strategic, and situationally defined expressions. While perhaps abstract to a fault, the view taken here is that accounting for context and the resulting strategy allows for the xenophobe to exist as a tangible and multifaceted entity. A model of this complexity is much better suited to contemporary societies in which mobility is common and interaction with strangers is an everyday event than simpler theories that do not account for unconscious expressions of intolerance. The multilayered model of xenophobic expression excludes unconditional statements. A person or group of people cannot be defined simply as xenophobic. The xenophobe acts strategically, raising the banner of intolerance openly in some circumstances, unconsciously in others, and not at all in still others. This flexible and adaptive view of the xenophobe offers agency and, moreover, avoids taking an essentialist approach to human behavior. Rather than a single expression of intolerance in a particular setting or time defining a person as a xenophobe, each and every expression of intolerance variously shapes how and to what extent the label "xenophobe" merits application.

2

THE STIGMA OF INTOLERANCE

THE DISCREDITABLE AND THE DISCREDITED INTOLERANTS

Equipped with a clear understanding of the multilayered model of the xenophobe, our theoretical focus now shifts to the xenophobe's motives. This transition was alluded to in the last chapter in the brief discussion of the determinants of the xenophobe's strategy of expression, which introduced the concept of social stigma. We will build upon more standard approaches to understand the determinants of antipathy and uncover why xenophobic expression shifts among layers. This is not an effort to see the emergence of xenophobia as a conversion process, in which a person finds new antipathy where none existed before. Instead, the goal here is to offer a clear mechanism by which the xenophobe elects for overt or covert expression, depending on the anticipated normative requirements of a social context. Again, the key mechanism is social *stigma*, which builds upon a well-defined theoretical tradition, although its application to the xenophobe requires some adaptation.

The person most associated with advancing our understanding of stigma is Erving Goffman. His fittingly titled work *Stigma* explores the implications and applications of the concept in everyday interactions.[1] The concept is fleshed out by contrasting the stigmatized with notions of normality, which is situationally determined. In other words, what is normal is what is expected in each social interaction, and this can change depending on the actors and context. This approach underlines how markers, often considered symbols, emerge in social interactions that can "spoil" efforts to manage how we are perceived by others. In essence, stigma is seen as a strategic mistake because its avoidance is an underlying motive for strategic behavioral adaptation. In short, stigma is to be avoided. To understand how one might go about doing this, Goffman conceived of a duality in which stigmatizing aspects of our identity are delineated by those that are revealed and those that are hidden: "The term stigma and its synonyms conceal a double perspective: does the stigmatized individual assume his [one's] differentness is known about already or is evident on the spot, or does he [one] assume it is neither known about by those present nor immediately perceivable by them? In the first case one deals with the plight of the *discredited*, in the second with that of the *discreditable*."[2]

To elucidate the implications of this "double perspective," let's consider a world where everyone is exactly as they appear. Granted, this has little to do with the world we live in but provides a useful, albeit hypothetical, starting point. In this proposed world, the xenophobe finds a religious or economic aspect of a stranger (i.e., a person about whom little is known) to be the target of antipathy and overtly expresses their aversion. This clinical way of describing the overt xenophobe can be translated into a less precise description: simply an openly bigoted person who, given the opportunity, let's you know it. If xenophobia is stigmatized, this type of expression leaves the xenophobe fully *discredited*. However, this label does not mean that all discredited forms of expression are to be avoided. Rather than a moral judgment, *discredited* defines an attribute, belief, or opinion that is revealed and as a result is observable by anyone involved in the interaction. Expressions of opinion or belief are in most instances optional. They emerge because of a preference (or poorly managed social strategy) but could easily be omitted—intentionally or unintentionally. However, *discredited* can also define phenotypic characteristics of an individual or group. To give an uninteresting example, the ability of a tall person to conceal one's height in a physical interaction is limited. As a result, an identity of "short" is unavailable to that individual, and, regardless of preferences, the label "tall" is applicable and plausibly applied. Tall stature is discredited.

The attitudes and behaviors of the xenophobe are obviously more consequential than an attribute like height. Unlike height, however, xenophobia (and most theoretically controversial beliefs) is easily masked. We can and often do restrain our expression depending on what the setting affords. This strategic approach to manage what others know of our opinions, beliefs, and preferences leaves much unsaid. As a result, the xenophobe's preferences and biases can easily remain *discreditable*. Their revelation is more of a strategic act, and the strategic advantage to keeping them hidden is to facilitate *passing*, which leaves others with a false impression that is advantageous for the xenophobe. Among the constellation of markers available to each of us, discreditable details are not obligatory, and we are free in many instances to elect never to share them. The distinction between the discredited and the discreditable is not pedantic. It is intimately linked to the anticipation of stigma—the strategic determinant of which layer of xenophobic expression best matches a particular context and situation. In a sense, navigating the discredited and discreditable dimensions of intolerance is the defining feature of the self-aware and strategic xenophobe. In the words of Goffman, "when the individual presents himself [one-self] before others, his [one's] performance will tend to incorporate and exemplify the officially accredited values of the society, more so, in fact, than does his [one's] behavior as a whole."[3]

Although a readily available option, a discreditable identity can require consistent maintenance for one's intolerant beliefs to remain unknown. This maintenance is a sort of active masking. Theoretically, sentiment like xenophobia is easily concealed and as such should require little effort to keep from others. Attributes like this are seen as "nicely invisible," and masking (i.e., passing) is a "matter of minor concern."[4] However, the fact that the xenophobe can remain discreditable is not quite as straightforward as it might first appear. In a dynamic context, in which attitudes toward immigrants, immigration, and ethnic, racial, and religious minorities are actively being negotiated and overlap, keeping xenophobia out of social interactions is far from simple. There are also reasons to share these beliefs to serve social and political ends. For example, some catalysts of social interactions in contexts such as political movements, national identity formation, evangelical forms of religious organization, and evolving demographic landscapes offer clear moments in which expression—covert or overt—is encouraged and in some cases required. Being stigmatized can be a form of group identity. If the profession of faith or voting behavior is motivated by concerns over the religious profile or policy implications of newcomers, the xenophobe would be incentivized to discredit themselves to rally a constituency or active public. The awareness of social stigma need not prevent this action and, depending on the oppositional nature of the group-level coordination, might encourage overt antipathy as a way to delineate membership.

That said, stigma and its avoidance do offer a clear way for us to understand how and why the xenophobe chooses to remain unknown in some contexts (i.e., layer 2 of the multilayered model). But stigma and its avoidance also underline the benefit of choosing and the incentive to prefer overt expression where circumstances permit. The xenophobe is constructed of overlapping layers that strategically vacillate between overt and covert expression. An individual can and often will mask some forms of xenophobic expression while overtly expressing others without hesitation. Both the overt and covert versions of the same xenophobic person are *true* in given contexts. For those who hold an intolerant view, the difference between what finds its way into an interaction and what remains masked depends on the anticipated social stigma of a defined social context. Put another way, stigma is defined by the context and defines the strategy.

This process is interpretative and far from infallible. The xenophobe might easily misjudge the situation and err in their strategic response—eliciting stigma without intention. However, the logic of a multilayered view of the xenophobe is that stigma (and its avoidance) shapes the choice, or strategy, of expression. A case in point is the United States, where opposition to citizenship for Christian and Muslim immigrants differed significantly so long as the xenophobe could expect social stigma for opposing co-religionists (i.e., Christians). In the absence of any risk of being stigmatized, opposition to Christian and Muslim immigrants no longer diverged.[5] However, there are also reasons to share these beliefs to serve social and political ends. Clearly, stigma matters and actively shapes how the xenophobe chooses to be presented, which skews our macro-level understanding of the prevalence of intolerance. In the chapters that follow, we will observe how the anticipation of stigma offers a mechanism of expression that explains the observed layering of the xenophobe. The key approach to uncovering masked intolerance is to provide a context in which stigma is no longer anticipated and a strategy of masking is therefore unnecessary. How? By the clever use of anonymity. This approach—simple to understand but somewhat difficult to apply—offers a pathway by which respondents can express stigmatizing attitudes and remain discreditable.

ANONYMITY AND STRATEGIES TO AVOID THE STIGMA OF INTOLERANCE

The fact that intolerance can be masked highlights a reality in which all is not always as it seems. Skepticism about the extent to which people openly express potentially stigmatizing views is a long-standing concern for scholars of attitudes and behavior and should be for all of us in our daily lives. Efforts to understand the dynamics of social interaction often embrace extended immersion and prolonged interaction or observation with an assumption that meanings are temporally, situationally, and relationally determined. This micro-level approach seeks to peel back the layers by establishing confidence between the observer and the observed. Some interpret this approach to imply that in many cases our understanding of social phenomena cannot be interpreted outside the context within which they were observed. This idea is somewhat irreconcilable with notions of reproducibility and generalizability, which are key to social inquiry.[6] Standard surveys are singled out as particularly problematic, which is reflected in the assertion that "public opinion polling gives an inaccurate and unrealistic picture of public opinion because of the failure to catch opinions as they are organized and as they operate in a functioning society."[7] Implicit in this statement about the primacy of situational logics is that the interaction itself shapes what is expressed. This is why distinct contexts elicit different strategies to avoid stigmatization. The approach taken here does not accept that macro-level insight is unattainable, nor does it accept that social phenomena are not defined by a particular context and moment. In other words, there is no reason to fully dismiss the need to measure and understand public sentiment, which provides macro-level findings that can be compared across time and geography. But the results are meaningful only if the context and the respondents' associated strategy of expression are fully taken into account. To do this such that the strategic response to stigma can be taken into account, which is a key element of effectively capturing the multilayered xenophobe, *anonymity* is crucial.

Stigma hates anonymity. Obviously, this is anthropomorphizing the term, but it does make the point. As any internet troll will attest, anonymity allows for some of the most toxic sentiment to be voiced (or typed) with little anticipation of accountability or social consequences. Specific terms (e.g., *doxing*[8]) have evolved to capture the loss of online anonymity. The gravity of having one's online persona discredited is reflected in the negative connotation the term elicits. The power of anonymity is that the force of the sentiment remains while the consequence of the sentiment—for the person expressing it—is managed and mitigated. Of course, anonymity as a tool to manage stigma is not limited to the empowerment of the prurient interest. Checks on repercussions for expressing an opinion undergird core civic acts like voting. The intention of the hidden ballot is to allow for support of a candidate to be decoupled from any individual consequences, whether it be stigmatization or physical or legal repercussions.

For the xenophobe, the first layer of expression is overt and, by definition, requires no guarantee of anonymity or other protection from social stigma. This point was made in chapter 1. Intolerance is openly expressed because there is no anticipation of stigma or because the fear of stigmatization is insufficient to warrant any change in behavior. Overt sentiment is easy enough to observe via standard survey methods and is certainly informative in its own way. There is no denying the ubiquity of such methods in social science and society more broadly. That said, considering overt xenophobic expression to be sufficient to understand who and to what extent intolerance is present provides a biased and limited view of the xenophobe. It is akin to judging an iceberg by what's visible above the water's surface. That can be a titanic error. To complete the picture, let's turn to the layers that are intentionally and unintentionally masked. These discreditable layers require the provision of anonymity and, moreover, the guarantee that it will hold.

Anonymity, afforded in an absolute and permanent way, reduces the threat of social stigma to the point that covert forms of xenophobic expression emerge. It is important that anonymity be understood to be assured beyond some notion of trust. In other words, handshake promises not to tell will not get the researcher far, particularly if the sentiment is likely to cause substantial social stigmatization. The approach used throughout this book leverages an experimental technique that has methodologically functioned to address the hesitancy with which controversial opinions are expressed. This hesitancy, frequently referred to as "social desirability bias," defines a well-known source of nonrandom error in measurement.[9] The perspective of the approach used in this book assumes that there is some absolute truth but that this truth is masked because of the pressure to present oneself desirably. For some details, this might be the case, particularly for behavioral outcomes. For example, mitigating social desirability bias has been used to obtain an improved estimate of the frequency of church attendance. Such details are factual rather than attitudinal, like xenophobia. As has been made clear, the multilayered model of the xenophobe acknowledges multiple versions of expression, each of which is true for a given context and interaction. In other words, the approach taken here is to reduce stigma via anonymity, but the interpretation is not that of a simple measurement correction. Why? Because covertly expressed xenophobic sentiment has no underlying, latent, or generalized attitudinal definition. Reducing stigma via anonymity offers a window into the second layer of xenophobic expression, but this is not some absolute view of what constitutes a xenophobe. Again, for discreditable attributes like attitudinal expression, a person can have multiple identities depending on the context and the strategy deployed. The xenophobe is no exception.

SOCIAL DESIRABILITY, SURVEY METHODS, AND IMPLICIT ASSOCIATIONS

An increasing body of work reveals the tendency of respondents to surveys (or any efforts to assess public opinion) to overreport tolerance toward a frequent target of xenophobia: migrants.[10] Research often highlights the fact that there is an observed reluctance or hesitancy to express behavior or values that might be interpreted as going against the prevailing norms of the context in which the survey is conducted. This reluctance, or social desirability bias, can—and often does—pattern responses. Although this bias is often interpreted as a nonrandom measurement error and baked into widely used theories of response behavior,[11] inherent in these findings is the implicit role of social stigma. Some work has even directly credited the anticipation of stigma with increasing respondents' reluctance to overtly express antipathy toward migrants. Before taking too deep a dive into the academic literature, largely rooted in survey methodology, an assumption needs to be made explicit. Most work targeting social desirability bias considers it to be akin to measurement error. The idea is that there is some fixed attitude and that responses shaped by social desirability bias are in a sense untrue. The multilayered model of the xenophobe highlights why this interpretation is limited at best. That said, the methods used to capture reluctantly expressed sentiment are insightful for understanding a multilayered model so long as the extent to which attitudes change in the presence of social stigma can be directly observed.

Work in survey methodology has long been confronted with the implications of the mode of interaction. In-person, online, and phone interviews can result in somewhat different response patterns for a given question, which is why consistency in the mode and wording of questions is crucial for retaining comparability between questionnaires administered to different people. The mode of collection can also affect response patterns for controversial topics. Certain modes of interaction can create more (e.g., online) or less (e.g., in person) social distance, but none offers the certainty of permanent and absolute anonymity. As a result, most survey data collection remains vulnerable to bias, which is widely acknowledged. Maintaining consistency in how a survey is administered reduces the variation in the known bias across observations (i.e., interviews). In sociology, some of the earliest efforts to understand the importance of social pressure to provide certain survey responses describe the pitfalls of interpreting controversial opinions in a straightforward manner.[12] The evidence for this phenomenon has only grown with time. Techniques suggested to mitigate the impact of social desirability bias have proliferated in survey methods and social science.[13] In work on migration, a frequent target of the xenophobe, social desirability bias has been determined to be the culprit for a pattern of bias in attitudes toward immigration policy or reform,[14] nativism,[15] and anti-immigrant sentiment.[16]

The presumption of explanations rooted in social desirability bias can border on normative, attributing measurement error to more general perspectives such as reasoned action.[17] One approach to address this concern is to deploy confirmatory factor analysis and bifactor models to control for social desirability tendencies.[18] This is really jargon, albeit well-meaning and informative jargon, that suggests that the use of more than one measure is useful when there is concern that some measures may result in biased results—regardless of the source of the bias. Emerging from this work is a menu of approaches that in essence seek to eliminate the reluctance, masking, hesitancy, or social desirability bias that may supress the overt expression of intolerant attitudes. Again, the focus is always on bias, which—either explicitly or implicitly—indicates an assumption that there is some latent truth that can be revealed. Some have taken to the unconscious (or subconscious), deploying implicit associations to measure attitudes. The basic idea for this approach is that people experience a greater cognitive load when evaluating associations that they do not find intuitive. Prejudicial attitudes will thus be uncovered if there is a delay in making associations, for example between positive words and migrant attributes.[19] These delays can be measured and the extent of the bias ascertained with a measure called the Implicit Association Test (IAT). Results from the IAT have been used to assesses attitudes toward migrants, identifying otherwise unmeasured antipathy in line with materialist theories of labor-market competition.[20] Sometimes the approach that focuses on the unconscious overlaps with social desirability bias, which is more a component of sentiment that is actively and intentionally expressed, but it is primarily intended to account for attitudes that are unknown (or actively denied) by the respondent.

THE LIST EXPERIMENT OR
ITEM-COUNT TECHNIQUE

As we've seen, efforts to measure public opinion have been concerned about the implications of social desirability for some time. In response, changes have been made to mode of interaction, and efforts to explore implicit attitudes have even been deployed, but success has varied. To be certain, there is value in these approaches, but the work here seeks to directly leverage the stigma that shapes the strategy of expression the xenophobe pursues. Rather than seeking to methodologically eliminate stigma, stigma can be used as a tool to explore different layers of expression—all of which are of interest. As subsequent chapters will empirically demonstrate, anonymity can offer respondents a context plausibly free of stigma within which to acknowledge support for unpopular opinions without inviting controversy. To accomplish this in each country context and subpopulation in which data were collected for this work, we deployed a simple and scalable counting measure termed the list experiment or item-count technique (ICT). In its most basic form, the design of the ICT presents two versions of a single survey question to two random samples of respondents. Many variations use more than two experimental groups or use multiple variations (i.e., frames) of a survey question. But for this introduction, let's limit the example to two random samples, which can be categorized by the standard labels of "treatment" and "control" (figure 2.1).

The first step in the list experiment is to present each experimental group, the participants of which are ideally randomly selected from a representative sample of some known population (e.g., citizens of the United States), with a list of items. Respondents are asked to state the number of items with which they agree or disagree. Alternatively, the questions could be about

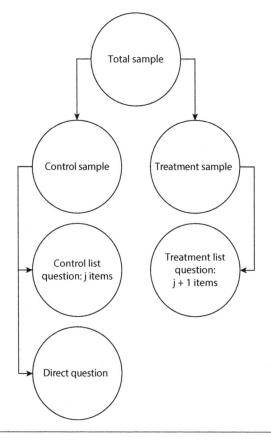

FIGURE 2.1 The list experiment or item-count technique

support or opposition for an issue. The content of the questions depends on what is intended to be measured. The key detail is that respondents indicate only the number of items that they support or agree with. For example, a control sample is given a list of items about providing assistance to the poor, taxation, and environmental regulation. The subject areas of the list items are not important so long as they are unrelated to the issue assumed to be subject to social stigmatization (e.g., xenophobia). A treatment group, also randomly selected from a representative sample of the same population, is offered an identical list of items but with one additional item that targets the focal issue—xenophobia in this case. Participants in both groups then identify just those items with which they agree or disagree or those they support or oppose.

It is crucial that the additional item, found only in the treatment list, is the *only* difference between the control and treatment list questions. Put in more technical terms, the control version of the question has j options, and the treatment version has j + 1 (see figure 2.1). Because both groups are presented the same list of items (j), any difference in the average response between the control and treatment groups results from the additional *focal* item presented to the treatment group. It then follows that subtracting the average response of the control group from the average response of the treatment group provides a measure of sentiment expressed under conditions of absolute and permanent anonymity. To offer greater clarity, consider a hypothetical case in which two identical people participate in a survey experiment. One receives the following control question and associated list of items:

The next questions are about your opinion on a few different issues in Ireland today. I am going to read out three things that you may or may not support. After I read all three, just tell me HOW MANY of them you support. I don't want to know which statements, just HOW MANY.

(1)   Higher weekly state pension
(2)   Lower tax on diesel
(3)   Bigger fines for litter

In this case, j equals three, and the hypothetical participant agrees with the first and third items, which results in a response of two. The participant in the treatment group receives a list with the same question but j + 1 items. The additional fourth item is the focal item in the list experiment and the outcome of interest in the manipulation. In this case, it is the following:

(4) More Polish people coming to live in Ireland

In this example, the respondent to the treatment list, defined as identical to the respondent to the control list (i.e., has the same preferences for two of the control list items), agrees with the focal item. The response for the treatment participant is thus three. Note that in each case, the preference of the respondent for any single item is not revealed and, in fact, cannot be known by the person who administers the survey experiment or has access to the individual responses at any point in the future. If we subtract the response to the control list question (i.e., two) from that to the treatment list question (i.e., three), we get one. In other words, we indirectly know the preferences of the respondent to the treatment list. Of course, this approach works only at the individual level because the two respondents are assumed to be identical, which is not plausible. Life is not that simple. In fact, when using this technique in real-world conditions, it is only the average response that is insightful.

To understand the power of averaging, imagine that we have two groups rather than two individuals. Instead of a single response, we can now calculate the average response across all respondents in either the treatment or control sample. So long as the two groups are random samples, observed and unobserved characteristics are equally represented in each group. As a result, the number that results from subtracting the average response to the control list question from the average response to the treatment list question is interpretable as the proportion who agree with the focal item. In the earlier example, rather than the exact preference for the focal item, this would be the overall proportion who support more Polish people coming to live in Ireland. In fact, the earlier example was taken from a real experiment that was fielded in 2019,[21] and the response to the control list question for a representative sample of the adult population of Ireland was 2.17 on average. For this list experiment, the response to the treatment list question was 2.70 on average. The difference between the two is 0.53, which can be converted to a percentage. The results thus indicate that 53 percent of Irish adults, or slightly more than half, supported more Polish people coming to live in Ireland.

At this point in the overview of the method, it is worth reiterating the importance of anonymity. This is how the list experiment sidesteps anticipated stigma: respondents state only a numeric response, thus avoiding any explicit indication of support or opposition for a specific item, let alone the focal item. One caveat is that the list of nonfocal items, which are all items in the control list, must elicit varied responses such that no individual fully agrees with or disagrees with all items. If a respondent endorses all items, anonymity cannot be maintained, and social stigma would remain relevant because the response to the focal item would be known. This is referred to as a "ceiling effect" and in the earlier example would have meant a response of four to the treatment list question. If the opposite is true and no items are endorsed, anonymity is similarly compromised in that the preference for the focal item again remains known; this is referred to as a "floor effect." In both instances, an assumption of anonymity would not hold, and the xenophobe would be discredited. So long as the number is not zero or equal to the number of all items (in this example, four), permanent anonymity remains guaranteed, and respondents can strategically avoid the stigma of expressing intolerance regardless of context.[22]

SOCIAL DESIRABILITY AND THE INTENTIONAL MASKING OF INTOLERANCE

At this point, we have identified the method by which social stigma can be accounted for, but it reveals response patterns only under the condition of anonymity. This method can conflate two distinct layers of xenophobic expression because there is nothing inherent in the manipulation—as described thus far—that differentiates those who would overtly express intolerance from those who would strategically mask their intolerance to avoid stigmatization. To untangle overt xenophobes from those who would prefer to remain discreditable requires the ability to compare their responses. To this end, a standard survey question would suffice because the response pattern captures *overt* support, which is ascertained in the absence of anonymity. Conveniently, average responses to direct questions can be directly compared to the difference between the average responses to the treatment and control questions. The result is interpretable as a measure of the extent to which xenophobia is masked (see figure 2.1).

For the control and treatment list questions used in the earlier example, the direct question would simply ask whether a respondent agrees or disagrees with the focal list item (i.e., more Polish people coming to live in Ireland). As no anonymity is available, the desire to avoid anticipated stigmatization could result in significant masking, assuming the context warrants such an expectation. In this case, the results would overreport support for migration defined as originating in Poland. When this question was asked in 2019 in Ireland, 73 percent of respondents agreed overtly with the direct question; that is, 20 percent more than the 53 percent ascertained via the list experiment. In other words, 20 percent of respondents indicated agreement only in the absence of anonymity. Clearly, being open to migrants from Poland is more likely to be expressed when overt sentiment is measured. Put another way, antipathy toward migrants from Poland is sometimes a covert act. In this example, the observed masking is significant and, moreover, substantive. If we were to limit our understanding of the xenophobe to overt expression, we would be left with the impression that nearly two-thirds of the Irish population support continued Polish immigration. This is a notably high level of support and, in the public square, accurately reflects discourse. However, the covert estimate suggests notably less tolerance. In some contexts, this disposition would be of greater relevance. Of course, neither is true in any absolute sense. Instead, with the approach outlined here, which will be used throughout this book, we can see both layers simultaneously. This method permits us to observe when and why some find it opportune to present intolerance. This approach and the variation it reveals fundamentally reshape what we understand a xenophobe to be.

This chapter offers a general introduction to the list experiment. All evidence that follows derives from the use of variations on this general design (see figure 2.1). There are adaptations, to be sure, which capture change over time and attitudes toward multiple out-groups. These variations reflect targeted and theoretically informed efforts to capture the context and adaptive strategy of the xenophobe in certain moments and contexts. For example, this technique was implemented before and after the financial crisis in the United States (chapter 3) and before and after the

Brexit referendum in the United Kingdom (chapters 4 and 6). Variations in treatment lists were pursued in Ireland and the Netherlands (chapters 5 and 6) and in Norway (chapter 7) to target distinct forms of xenophobia. In each case, the fundamental goal remained the same: to model the xenophobe as a contextually defined strategic actor. The removal of stigma and the resultant change in responses does not (and cannot) reveal the true xenophobe. Instead, the list experiment—when compared with a direct measure—offers a straightforward, scalable, and easily interpretable way to capture the two distinct outer layers of the multilayered model of xenophobic expression. Using this method, we can assess the strategy used by the xenophobe to navigate a defined context. Doing so permits us to directly observe the implications that varying, contextually determined degrees of stigma have for our multilayered understanding of the xenophobe.

A NOTE ON SELF-DECEPTION AND UNCONSCIOUS BIASES

The list experiment offers unique insight, but some dimensions of the xenophobe remain obscured. The technique distinguishes strategically masked xenophobic expression from that which is overtly articulated. But it *cannot* account for unconscious manifestations of antipathy, which reside in the third, innermost layer of the multilayered model of xenophobic expression (see figure 0.1 in the introduction). These unconscious forms of intolerance remain unacknowledged regardless of the level of anonymity provided. They are unknown to the respondent, and as a result the anticipation of social stigma is not relevant. As mentioned earlier, there are empirical approaches that seek to capture forms of intolerance that might not be known even to the person holding the biases. The standard approach is the IAT,[23] which, as mentioned, measures the time participants take to make associations between words or images. When measuring a concept like xenophobia, participants are asked to associate positive and negative evaluations with immigrant and nonimmigrant attributes. A greater delay in making associations between positive evaluations and immigrant attributes would be interpreted as reflecting negative unconscious bias.

This approach has been critiqued[24] and defended[25] in the literature. Despite its drawbacks, it remains in widespread use as a reproducible and empirically sound measure of unconscious intolerance. However, unlike the ICT used here, it does not distinguish between layers of xenophobic expression or address the role of social stigma. It serves better as a catch-all measure of the xenophobe that groups overt and covert—conscious and unconscious—forms of expression into a single dimension. If preferences revealed by the IAT differ from individuals' articulated preferences, the gap is attributed to the participant either being unaware or deceptive. The latter implies volition, whereas the former implies an unconscious act. The unique contribution of this work remains the revelation and identification of the type of xenophobe who uses the expression of tolerance as a strategy to navigate social interactions. The approach taken here does not discount the importance of self-deception as a mechanism by which unconscious intolerance is perpetuated. In fact, unconscious bias has received notable attention in the academic literature in recent years. However, the strength of the survey experiment design used throughout this book is its ability to distinguish covert and overt forms of intolerance that are strategic in nature and conscious (i.e., intentional) in their manifestation.

II

ECONOMIC POPULISM AND THE POLITICS OF XENOPHOBIC EXPRESSION

3

IF THERE ARE NO DOGS, WHY WHISTLE?

Intolerance and the Xenophobic Seeds of Populism

MATERIALIST THEORIES OF ANTI-IMMIGRANT SENTIMENT

Economic concerns, fundamentally material in nature, are theorized to be a core motive of xenophobic sentiment. The mechanism, often measured by the rate of unemployment or a change in wages, is the perception of newcomers as a source of economic competition or threat. The rationale is that a national economy is (or should be) managed primarily for the benefit of resident, nonmigrant workers. If that brief description seems nationalistic, it is no accident. Undergirding materialist theories of anti-immigrant sentiment is a nativist understanding that economic benefits are both finite and primarily for those with greater attachment to a national context. Although definitions of those who are more (or less) deserving of access and mobility in a labor market may vary, the key theoretical detail is that the concerns about migrants are independent of sociocultural narratives. Instead, materialist-driven perspectives conceptualize xenophobes as "rational actors, natives pursuing their own well-being [who] develop unfavorable attitudes to legitimate their social positions when competing with foreigners over jobs . . . , especially during times of economic recession."[1] This broad claim is rooted in three suppositions, each of which requires definitional clarity if materialist theories are to remain plausible, relevant, and operationalizable perspectives on xenophobic sentiment.

First, the materialist perspective requires that the xenophobe clearly distinguish migrant from nonmigrant labor. Even this seemingly straightforward detail necessitates a categorization of convenience to create a division rigid enough to bifurcate an entire economic context. Typically, a migrant-versus-nonmigrant division delineates economic claims to primacy using citizenship, birth, or some defined duration of residency. None of these is coherent in all instances because some contexts retain multigenerational residents who are excluded from citizenship. An example is some members of the Korean community in Japan who have not been naturalized or conferred citizenship to their descendants after decades of residence.[2] Other contexts do not distinguish migrants who might have completed a process of naturalization from those who access the labor market only via other types of permission (e.g., long-term residential work permits, spousal residency permissions). An example of this approach has been followed by my own institution, University College Dublin, where, regardless of subsequent naturalization, employees not originally from Ireland are considered non-Irish when internationalization, which is viewed positively, is quantified for rankings.[3] This accounting approach allows an institution never to lose a migrant academic via naturalization or duration of residence. Conversely, neither duration of residence nor acquisition of citizenship can ever increase the pool of domestic workers.

Second, the materialist view dictates that migrants must constitute real competition in the labor market. Again, the details are crucial if the perception of material threat is to remain plausible. Overgeneralizations rooted in blanket assumptions that any newcomer to an economy is perceived as competition are untenable because they shift the theoretical perspective more toward sociocultural or identity-based motives. A recent overview of the literature points out inconsistent findings when actual threat is measured, suggesting that a more nuanced perspective is needed to clearly show whether nonnative competition is really an underlying concern.[4] In search of contexts in which a realistic threat is plausible, some have homed in on specific sectors of the economy, finding that workers who experience economic uncertainty in the moment or anticipate it in the foreseeable future are less inclined to support migrants or migration.[5] When considering realistic threat, two characteristics of the nonmigrant population are frequently used to identify the workers (or the unemployed) most plausibly affected by the arrival of potential competition: education and wages.

Education, which is used as a proxy for skills, is interpreted as a marker of labor-market position. Education, which is included in most surveys and other efforts to gauge public opinion, is accurately reported for the most part and, on the surface, appears informative. The common finding is that opposition to migrants and migration is more prevalent among the less educated.[6] The prevailing interpretation of this frequently observed pattern is that less-skilled workers compete more directly with migrants than those who are more highly skilled. The key assumption here is that migrants, for the most part, are similarly skilled to the less educated or, at the start, are employed in jobs that don't require large amounts of human-capital investment. As a result, assuming this perception of newcomers is held, migrants constitute realistic, direct competitors for work or wages for the less-skilled native labor force.

The standard interpretation of education is not without problems. As with the ambiguity about who constitutes a migrant within a defined national economy, the use of education creates interpretive uncertainty because it also has implications for the xenophobe's strategic navigation of anticipated social stigma associated with the expression intolerance. Strategy, as we've come to understand, is a core component of the multilayered model of xenophobic expression. The implications are clear: the more educated—among whom the xenophobe is found to be notably less prevalent—are also plausibly more *reluctant* to express antipathy toward migrants. That hesitancy would predict a shift from overt to covert expression rather than denoting greater tolerance in some absolute sense. If this is the case, the materialist interpretation of education is less viable. There is evidence (some of which is included in this book) of a sincere shift away from an interpretation of education as a simple proxy for skills, but the materialist interpretation remains prevalent and widely accepted. The continued acceptance of the materialist perspective is unfortunate because without xenophobic expression being understood as a multilayered phenomenon, there is a real risk of conflating significant masking with materialist interpretations of educational gradients, which presents a biased view of the xenophobe.

Wages provide a second front where material needs are posited to evolve into a realistic perception of threat. Rather than hinging on competition—real or perceived—for employment, the wage argument centers on a spatially defined labor market (e.g., national, regional) holding a lower reservation wage in which an influx of newcomers would lower the wages for all workers competing for work in a particular occupation. From this perspective, wages are understood to erode for all if there is an available pool of workers who will work for less, and this group is understood to be migrants. The most widely cited example of this phenomenon in the literature is work by Borjas and colleagues, who conclude that some cohorts of migrants to the United States caused wages to decline in some contexts.[7]

As with education, materialist concerns rooted in wages are sometimes hard to reconcile with the reality of contemporary migration. One issue is the extent to which the implications for wages of an influx of workers is known or easily interpretable by autochthonous members of a defined labor market. Although there might be an empirical case in which wages are lowered if employers recognize that migrant applicants will work for less, is this something that other workers understand and, more importantly, use as a rationale to sustain xenophobia? This invites a broader question. Does a macro-level change in the composition of workers (or the population more broadly) alter individual-level perceptions of migration at all?

Third, competition in the labor market must be seen as a realistic concern or threat. Verifying a realistic perception of threat is crucial because core theories of intergroup conflict, backed by empirical evidence, indicate that between-group tension—even between groups with minimal attachment—emerges only when conflict is perceived as a realistic outcome.[8] This is a particularly tricky aspect when defining plausible material motives for xenophobia. Although competition for employment or wages seems like a believable motive and, in certain contexts, may be objectively true, such competition is unlikely to motivate the xenophobe unless labor-market outcomes are credibly perceived as having been degraded by newcomers. Conversely, a perception of realistic threat need not be rooted in any actual economic impact. The material consequences of migration for the labor market are potentially immaterial. The xenophobe could perceive a material threat as realistic even in the absence of any objective erosion in employment opportunities or wages. This pattern is a form of economic populism, reflecting a coupling of economic nationalism and nativism, potentially untethered from objective macro-level patterns in employment and wages.

It is insightful that evidence for materialist determinants of xenophobic sentiment is decidedly mixed. Even with some work showing an objective impact on the labor market such as a decline in wages, the link with a perception of threat by the nonmigrant population and, moreover, the evolution of this perception into an expression of xenophobic sentiment are far from certain. In fact, when considering broad arguments about materialist determinants of xenophobia, the core assumption that those with skill levels assumed to be disproportionately affected by immigration are the same people who harbor greater xenophobia struggles for support in the literature. Some work has gone as far as to conclude that the materialist perspective, summarized as labor-market competition theory, should be eliminated as a core factor in the patterning of xenophobic sentiment in the United States[9] and Europe[10] because it does not seem to drive opposition.[11]

In contrast, some work focusing on the pattern of observed income[12] or average occupational wages[13] has found that lower wages do indeed predict greater opposition to immigration. This finding does not offer insight into the perception of threat, but it is suggestive. However, others remain less convinced and suggest that there is limited support for this notion and that no blanket assumption about wages and immigration holds up to scrutiny.[14] When the individual-level perception of workers is taken into account, the evidence is also inconclusive, with expectations of reduced wages or lower income failing to translate into greater opposition to migration.[15] The key takeaway from this discussion is that assumptions about who will be affected by migrant labor (e.g., the unskilled, the highly educated, the service sector) must be made clear before arguments about materialist motives

for xenophobia can be deemed applicable. In addition, the possibility that some proxies of economic position (e.g., being highly
educated) might strategically avoid the stigma of intolerance has
implications for the interpretation of xenophobia in a stratified
labor market. Clearly, it is not obvious and should not be taken
for granted that the experience of competition, real or perceived,
creates more xenophobes or, conversely, that the absence of competition results in fewer.

"THE LIFEBOAT IS FULL" AND OTHER WAYS TO AVOID THE STIGMA OF SOCIOCULTURAL INTOLERANCE

Despite mixed evidence that materialist concerns determine
xenophobia, the theoretical bridge linking anti-immigrant sentiment to material precarity is widely cited.[16] A wry observation
of the persistence of materialist perspectives of xenophobia is
reflected in a somewhat recent review of the literature in which
it is labeled a "zombie theory" because it lives on, presumably
aimlessly shuffling from one policy debate to another, with little
empirical support.[17] Despite this seeming dismissal of the notion
that materialist concerns drive antipathy toward migrants, some
remain emphatically unconvinced and continue to conclude
that "perceptions of economic threat are a crucial driving factor
behind negative attitudes toward immigration."[18]

This book offers an alternative view—a third way perhaps.
Instead of materialist concerns being a *driver* of xenophobic
sentiment, the evidence presented here suggests that the logic of
economic threat offers a less stigmatized avenue through which
intolerance can be expressed. Put another way, it is a mechanism
by which stigma can be avoided, thus allowing a shift from covert

to open expressions of intolerance. To link this strategic change to the multilayered model, xenophobes shift antipathy from the second layer to the first when materialist concerns are available and socially acceptable—regardless of any realistic impact of migrant labor. Focusing on the determinants of xenophobic *expression*, rather than some general underlying mechanism, is more than a semantic shift. It has concrete implications for some interpretations of observed trends in anti-immigrant sentiment or support for restrictive immigration policy.

Put succinctly, if materialist concerns reduce stigma, overt support can emerge without being propelled by an overall change in perspective. It is no longer required that materialist concerns convert individuals into xenophobes. Instead, these concerns change how xenophobia is expressed, which is a very different matter. In this scenario, materialist concerns are better understood a means by which the xenophobe can avoid the stigma of sociocultural motives like racism and religious bigotry. Examples to consider are economic crises in which materialist logics are pushed to the foreground. These moments offer a clear test of the extent to which eroding material circumstances translate into an increase in the prevalence of overt xenophobia. When economic precarity is rising, the rationale of materialist concerns is more available and accepted, regardless of whether the sense of threat is driven by an actual increase in unemployment or erosion of wages. To translate this perspective into the multilayered view of the xenophobe, an exogenous economic shock (i.e., an external event that affects us but offers us no say in the matter) provides a serendipitous decline in the stigma of materialist arguments against migrant workers or further migration.

Consider the analogy of the lifeboat, which is often used by those claiming the logic of material precarity. The material threat is exemplified by the finite size of the boat on which we are hypothetically adrift. The size of the boat is determined by the carrying capacity of a defined economy—typically national but possibly composed of multiple states (e.g., the European Union). Too many passengers will sink the boat or reduce the rations available. There is typically an allusion to some survival drama. The argument against new passengers (i.e., migrants) becomes impersonal in this scenario. It is not that any one person is targeted for exclusion. It is simply that the boat is full. Any additional passengers would threaten the well-being of those already aboard.

This analogy is revealing because it suggests that materialist concerns do not target newcomers because of their differences per se—aside from arriving late—but are instead an unfortunate necessity and a reflection of a cold economic reality. It removes agency from the xenophobic narrative because the intolerance is rooted in a concern that is presented as objective and outside any individual's control. No sociocultural concerns need be offered because the xenophobe relies on an economic out-group that is defined by the materialist concerns of those already having access to a particular economic context. Other attributes such as race, religion, ethnicity, and nativity—aside from those affecting the economic flavor inherent in the ideal of a national economy—are not relevant so long as the threat is limited to the material. If mentioned at all, nonmaterial attributes that might define targeted newcomers are treated as an accident of timing and place. The stigma that they might elicit as indicative of racism, Islamophobia, ethnocentrism, or nativism, although potentially anticipated, can be avoided. In fact, the stigmatization of nonmaterial manifestations of intolerance might act as a catalyst for material considerations to be presented as more salient.

Now that we are acquainted with the multilayered model of the xenophobe, upticks in overt sentiment—even those linked to a perception of economic precarity—need not be interpreted as indicative of a general increase in the prevalence of xenophobia. It is equally plausible that the observed increase in overt antipathy represents a shift between layers of expression. This perspective is quite different from the traditional materialist logic that suggests that an increase in overt intolerance requires an actual change in sentiment at the individual level. As mentioned, this nuance is more than semantic. If we adopt this view, we see that a greater prevalence of xenophobia in the wake of an economic downturn is caused by a shift from masked, covert forms of expression to unmasked, overt forms of expression, which represents a convenient strategic option rather than a true increase in intolerance explained by a materialist theory. Let's consider a concrete case.

THE UNITED STATES: AN ECONOMIC CRISIS AS AN EXCUSE FOR OVERT XENOPHOBIA

The United States presents an interesting case that coupled a prolonged economic recession with a notable increase in the prevalence of overtly xenophobic rhetoric in national politics, which some conclude were intertwined.[19] The recent—albeit not the most recent—financial crisis of 2007–2008 offers a unique window into the role of economic concerns in shaping xenophobic expression because the rapid and pronounced downturn resulted in an extraordinary spike in unemployment. The shock to the economy was rapid, causing workers to see their earnings and prospects for future employment diminish, which had implications for individual debt like mortgages. The material precarity of the moment was coupled with the spectacular collapse of the subprime mortgage market beginning in late 2007. The result was an unprecedented intervention by the U.S. Federal Housing Finance Agency, which placed the guarantors of the bulk of U.S. home mortgages—the Federal Home Loan Mortgage Corporation (known as Freddie Mac) and the Federal National Mortgage Association (known as Fannie Mae)—under federal conservatorship. Private banks were similarly buffeted, and it became clear that the crisis was uniquely lethal when Lehman Brothers, a 158-year-old holding company and investment bank, declared bankruptcy. This precise moment is considered by many to be the start of the prolonged financial crisis that came to define the Great Recession of the subsequent decade.[20]

Predictably, the economic downturn did not affect everyone to the same degree. Existing inequities were further exacerbated, and certain sectors of the population were disproportionately negatively affected. One way to see this clearly is to consider patterns in unemployment by completed level of education, as shown in figure 3.1. The monthly trend in the seasonally adjusted unemployment rate shows a notable expansion of inequalities after the onset of the crisis, reflected in a fanning out of the trend lines by level of completed education in the postcrisis period. Granted, workers at every level of education experienced some increase in unemployment after the meltdown, but the least educated were hit the hardest (as shown by the notably steeper gradient in figure 3.1). To put this finding in perspective, the unemployment rate of the most educated peaked at about 5 percent after the financial crisis, whereas the least educated were at that level during the boom times before the crisis. The best of times for the least educated is equivalent to the worst of times for the most educated. Of course, the financial crisis is not the only relevant factor to consider in this case. Migration is always part of the national conversation on some level in

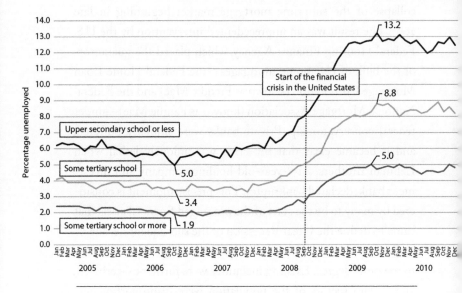

FIGURE 3.1 Patterns in pre- and postcrisis unemployment
by level of education

Source: Adapted from Mathew J. Creighton, Amaney Jamal, and
Natalia C. Malancu, "Has Opposition to Immigration Increased in the United States After
the Economic Crisis? An Experimental Approach," *International Migration Review* 49,
no. 3 (2015): 727–56.

the United States, reflected in a perpetually contested effort at
immigration reform[21] and the mobilization of large rallies in
favor of migrant rights in the period that proceeded the crisis.

The rapid and widely understood erosion of the U.S. economy
presents a clear-cut moment in which economic precarity comes
sharply into focus. The materialist perspective sees these exogenous shocks, which are outside of any individual's control, as
opportune moments to observe the creation of xenophobes who
perceive newcomers as competition for jobs and wages, which is
reflected in a more overtly hostile view. Migrants become available targets because materialist concerns are shared by all; in

these conditions, a case can be made that intolerance is expressed as a reaction to material threat rather than any particular attributes of the newcomers. The expected outcome is a rise in overtly expressed opposition to migration, particularly in areas and among groups disproportionately affected by an economic downturn. This assumption is deeply embedded in the way economic crises are seen to shape electoral politics and public opinion in the United States, particularly as a motive for increased support for more authoritarian flavors of governance. The years immediately after the financial crisis have seen a move toward political populism, particularly in areas that were economically hard hit and included a labor force seen as sensitive to less-skilled migrant labor.[22] A political shift in the Rust Belt is notable given the area's postindustrial labor force, which historically had been part of a political coalition that favored relatively more inclusive policy positions on migration. This shift is broadly encapsulated in the rise of a brand of right-wing populism that embraced a strident and overt antiimmigrant message.[23] How does a multilayered view of the xenophobe help us understand these trends? The answer lies in whether the postcrisis period created new xenophobes or only reduced the need to mask existing xenophobia—thereby making the xenophobe visible.

CHANGING MINDS OR CHANGING NORMS?

Now that the stage is set, let's directly test the importance of materialist concerns in shaping intentionally masked intolerance. As a starting point, it helps to be deliberately naive. Let's assume that there is no layering in the mind of the xenophobe. There is no strategic expression of intolerance. Social stigma is irrelevant, and xenophobia in any context is always overtly expressed and easily observed. The late 2007 wobble and early 2008 collapse of the U.S. economy—not to mention the chain reaction globally—and the ensuing jump in unemployment present a clear case for lifeboat logic. Those who found migrant contribution to the labor market unremarkable or even beneficial suddenly found that what was seen as complementary (or even beneficial) had turned into potential competition. The ship might have had berths, but the lifeboat is now clearly full.

Of course, this perspective is implausible at best and intentionally deceptive at worst. But if we ignore that for the moment, we can try to understand why the materialist perspective is so compelling. However, we cannot limit our view of the xenophobe only to overt forms of expression. Instead, we will use an approach that also permits us to observe intentionally and consciously masked xenophobes. Chapter 2 introduced a method, adopted throughout this book, that permits the sentiment of overt xenophobes to be contrasted with the identical sentiment expressed under conditions of absolute and permanent anonymity. Without too much repetition, it is useful to recall how the list experiment works. We will first look at the pattern of responses to questions about a closed border in the United States asked before the financial crisis. We will then consider the pattern of responses to the same questions asked after the crisis had unfolded. The question was asked in different ways, allowing for treatment and control conditions, and distinct levels of anonymity were provided to respondents. Put a different way, the experimental design permitted the stigma of intolerance to be mitigated in some circumstances but not in others. The result was a direct view into the extent to which stigma shaped what was overtly expressed and how such expression changed in response to materialist considerations, which were clearly different before and after the onset of the financial crisis. These data were collected in collaboration

TABLE 3.1 OVERT AND COVERT OPPOSITION TO A CLOSED U.S. BORDER: BEFORE AND AFTER THE FINANCIAL CRISIS

	Before 2005	After 2010	Difference 2005–2010
Percentage overtly opposed to closing the U.S. border	60%*	43%*	17%*
Percentage covertly opposed to closing the U.S. border	32%*	31%*	1%
Percentage masking their opposition (overt–covert)	28%*	12%*	
Participants	473	793	

Source: Mathew J. Creighton and Amaney Jamal, "Perceptions of Islam, Migration and Citizenship in the United States: A List Experiment," Time-Sharing Experiments for the Social Sciences, 2010, https://www.tessexperiments.org/study/creighton022; Alexander L. Janus, "The List Experiment as an Unobtrusive Measure of Attitudes Toward Immigration and Same-sex Marriages," OSF Registries (2015), https://doi.org/10.17605/OSF.IO/4HQBW;

Note: The overt question was worded as follows: "Do you support or oppose cutting off all immigration to the United States?" The covert question was worded similarly but administered such that opposition did not require overt expression. (See chapter 2 for a more detailed description of the technique and appendix 1 for the full text of all questions). In the table, * indicates that the reported percentage is significantly different from zero (p ≥ 0.05).

with Amaney Jamal, and a more technical description of some of the results described in this chapter was published in 2015 with Natalia Malancu as coauthor (see appendix 1 for a detailed overview of the experimental design).[24]

Table 3.1 offers a succinct view of how masked intolerance distorts our understanding of the materialist motives underpinning xenophobia.[25] The first row reflects the naive view of things. This is a deliberate straw man. Before the financial crisis, about an estimated 60 percent of the U.S. population were opposed to a closed border. In other words, 40 percent expressed no opposition to effectively ending immigration, an admittedly extreme position given the country's history. Depending on one's preconceived ideas about the extent to which the United States is a welcoming context, this pattern is either expected or surprising.

The table also shows that the percentage overtly opposed to closing the U.S. border fell to 43 percent after the crisis, a decline of 17 percentage points—nearly one-fifth of the estimated population—during the same period that unemployment increased dramatically (see figure 3.1). This pattern has been observed in other work using overt public opinion in which individuals were asked about the impact of migration on the U.S. economy before and after the financial crisis.[26] In addition, this change in the percent opposed is significant[27] and, without an understanding of the multilayered reality of the xenophobe, would indicate that economic precarity does indeed translate into hostility toward migration. However, the second row, which reveals the covert xenophobe, tells a substantively different story. A multilayered view clearly matters.

Now that we've got a sense of the naive, overt view, let's move beyond it to consider the implications of context and strategy: the two key elements of a multilayered model of the xenophobe. Using anonymity, we were able to observe the precrisis levels of covert opposition to a closed border. The clear majority evaporated: just under one-third of the estimated U.S. population found a closed border to be worth opposing. This is a change of 28 percent, which is substantive and significant difference. After the financial crisis, a similar pattern was observed. The 43 percent who expressed overt opposition was reduced to 31 percent, a decline of 12 percent, which, as with the precrisis period, indicates a substantive and significant change (see the third row of table 3.1). The real insight here emerges when the precrisis period is compared with what follows. Covertly expressed opposition was nearly unchanged: from 32 percent before the crisis to 31 percent afterward. The 31 percent result was found during the same period in which unemployment more than doubled and overt opposition declined by 17 percent. The overt and covert xenophobe are not the same and should not be conflated.

What should we take away from these findings? These results bring to foreground the fact that a population-level shift in the extent to which those who openly express xenophobic sentiment anticipate stigma can (and does) change. The interpretation of this change is where the multilayered view really deviates from that based only on overt expression. Instead of materialist concerns changing people's minds in some absolute sense, the pattern of overt and covert expression demonstrate that the xenophobe is strategic and that economic crises can offer an opportunity to express xenophobia more openly. That perspective is different from one that attributes some causal and mechanistic interpretation to materialist concerns such that they are a deterministic driver of intolerance. They might be a motive but only for choosing overt expression. Evidence suggest that materialist concerns are not interpretable as affecting a change in perspective on migration in all contexts and interactions. The covert and overt layers of the xenophobe exist in parallel and neither can be claimed to be more (or less) reflective of reality.

Another insight from these findings is that the second, covert layer of the multilayered model of the xenophobe, defined by intentional and strategic masking, can be relatively stable during notably turbulent economic vacillations. Moreover, far more intolerance can be expressed at this layer than what might be interpreted from intolerance expressed at the first, overt layer. It is worth considering that opposition to a closed border was lower before the financial crisis when expressed covertly than after the crisis when expressed overtly (32 percent versus 43 percent). One could delve further into these patterns to extract greater detail about the changes in overt and covert expression by other attributes,[28] but the story remains the fundamentally unchanged. A dramatic change in material circumstances, defined by the largest economic crisis in recent memory, did not lead to any substantive or significant change in intentionally masked xenophobia in the United States, which was the epicenter of the financial meltdown. Although materialist considerations, summarized by the lifeboat argument, do shape overt xenophobic expression, they determine the strategy of opposition to immigration rather than its underlying cause.

POSTCRISIS POPULISM AND XENOPHOBES AS A CONSTITUENCY

It is helpful at this point to ground the implications of a multilayered xenophobe in a concrete social and political context. Borders, immigration, and opposition to immigration became a core theme in U.S. electoral politics following the financial crisis. This does not mean that immigration is a new topic in U.S. politics—far from it[29]—but the change in sentiment following the onset of the financial crisis does provide a unique opportunity to observe differences in overt and covert forms of xenophobic expression. The feature that has come to define the postcrisis political landscape in the United States is the emergence of xenophobes as a visible constituency. The covert xenophobe, embodying an unspoken reservoir of intolerance that table 3.1 clearly highlights, remained nearly unchanged throughout the crisis. Materialist concerns legitimized by economic precarity resulted in a rise in xenophobic expression at only one layer: the overt one. The Great Recession converted xenophobes into a visible and targetable electorate, which U.S. populism discovered could be advantageous.

In times of economic stability, economic prosperity limits the legitimacy of xenophobic sentiment. The ability of political campaigns and candidates to embrace xenophobic rhetoric is thereby hindered because the link between intolerance and nonmaterialist attributes of newcomers is clear. Political strategy can hardly isolate economic hardship in a booming economy. Moreover, polling data are unlikely to reflect the resonance of xenophobia as a political motivator because the anticipation of stigma for overtly expressing intolerance would be strategically unappealing to many respondents. Political strategy would not and could not anticipate a benefit. Instead, the xenophobe—whether it be the candidate, the campaign, or the potential constituent—would appear to be better served by pursuing a less controversial campaign issue. In the precrisis United States, the xenophobe would have needed to signal intolerance covertly. One way to understand covertly expressed intolerance is to think of a dog whistle, whose sound can be heard only by a specific audience and a historical mainstay of race-based politics in the United States. However, the precrisis dog whistle became clearly audible by 2010.

In the postcrisis United States, the lifeboat argument could have been used as a rationale for intolerance independent from intolerance based on other attributes because an easily observed deterioration in economic conditions was the most salient contextual feature for most and was widely understood. The reduction in anticipated stigma opened the door to the outspoken populist rhetoric that increased in volume and experienced notable success in attracting support and identifying candidates.[30]

In short, materialist concerns provided a way to narrow the interpretation of xenophobia. Immigration is now an economic issue, and as such sociocultural concerns (e.g., race, ethnicity, religion) are of no consequence. Once the xenophobe is understood as a multilayered agent who emerges when strategically viable, the "shift" observed in the extent to which the xenophobe elects overt expression becomes decoupled from a change in mindset.

Stigmatized contexts can also provide opportunities for xenophobes to organize, politically and socially. I don't mean to imply that the precrisis United States was more tolerant in any absolute sense than it was following the onset of the crisis. The point made here is that the xenophobe confronts a landscape where the presentation of intolerance is not straightforward. The expression of intolerance requires just the right pitch to avoid the easily anticipated stigma that in-group preferences based on sociocultural preferences would elicit—at least in the United States. The logic of the lifeboat can dominate a context in moments of economic strain. This narrowing of the gap between the first (overt) and second (covert) layers of the multilayered model of xenophobic expression creates the conditions for an increase in a flavor of populism that embraces a more vocal, strident, and vociferous animosity directed toward migrants and migration. What we can learn from this pattern is that political opportunity defines economic crises. The adage "never let a good crisis go to waste" is clearly pertinent. Populism takes advantage of a changed context and adapts its strategy accordingly, but the xenophobe is not the inventor of this new contextual reality. Instead, populism is political opportunism and as such should find a less welcoming climate in times of economic prosperity despite the covert prevalence of xenophobes remaining unchanged.

4

REFERENDA AND BORDERS

Brexit and the Role of the Xenophobe in
the Division of Europe

The last chapter showed that material concerns act as a pathway to destigmatize xenophobic expression, allowing the overt xenophobe greater freedom to strategically maneuver a social context of interaction. An economic shock makes precarity in terms of employment or wages even more salient and, evidence suggests, reduces the need to strategically mask intolerance. This understanding is essentially a top-down perspective. Although the policy missteps that resulted in the subprime mortgage market expanding and rapidly collapsing are human in origin, the intention of these events was not to embolden the xenophobe—that emboldening was just an opportunistic result of strategic behavior. The alignment of an economic shock with an increase in overt xenophobia has resulted in the often erroneous privileging of materialist theories in our understanding of the motives for xenophobia. In this chapter, we'll consider a more intentional change in context. The objective is to understand how intentional efforts to mobilize, socially and politically, around the issue of borders influence the xenophobe. Specifically, we'll trace how multiple layers of xenophobic expression react to political rhetoric. The best and most recent example for doing so is the referendum that took the United Kingdom out of the European Union: Brexit.

Borders—or the lack thereof—are at the heart of the European Union. From its inception, the European Union has framed the free movement people and goods as two sides of the same coin.[1] This notion was accepted by most EU member states, with some variation,[2] as well as by several neighboring states (e.g., Norway). The result is a near-frictionless ability to cross borders within the European Union and, as a result, a significant flow of EU residents among member states.[3] One obvious consequence is the erosion of the distinction between domestic and international migration—at least from a legal perspective. The ease of migration within the European Union has not been met with universal acceptance, particularly among some constituencies in EU members states. Although many find free physical movement within the European Union to translate into other forms of upward social and economic mobility, some interpret the intentional de-emphasis of state borders as a threat to national sovereignty.[4]

It is undeniable that certain EU states are more popular destinations than others. Marquee events, like the expansion of the European Union to include some larger sending countries (e.g., Poland, Romania) coupled with a somewhat rapid increase in refugee migration in latter half of the 2010s, resulted in tensions among some members states. In the case of refugee migration, the issue became the obligation of EU states to settle refugees and the re-emergence of national borders to prevent the free movement of refugees within the European Union as a temporary intervention rooted in single-state, national interest. As the European Union has expanded and negotiated border concerns, the rank order of importance placed on migration as an issue has increased.[5] This context sets the stage for migration becoming a persistent fixture of electoral politics within EU member states. Debates often center on the role of the European Union in exacerbating material concerns as new workers compete for jobs.

Sociocultural concerns are also on the radar because new arrivals face no barriers to long-term settlement, and contexts of origin, particularly for refugee migration, can be outside contemporary definitions of Europe or bordering non-EU states. If there is one event that encapsulates these tensions, it's Brexit.

THE VIEW FROM ABOVE: THE DISCOURSE OF ELITE XENOPHOBES

Before digging into the case of Brexit, let's consider a broader question: Does political rhetoric shape distinct layers of xenophobic expression? The theoretical issue, at its core, is the role of political elites in legitimizing certain views—in this case, intolerance. As with materialist concerns, highlighted in the previous chapter, the multilayered model of xenophobic expression accounts for the important role that *shifts* in contextual norms play in increasing or decreasing the anticipated stigma of certain xenophobic frames. In the case of the financial crisis in the United States, the contextual shift did not involve a notable amount of agency. It was more the result of an opportunistic strategic response to heightened concern about material precarity. Elite discourse shines a light on how the xenophobe navigates contextual norms in moments when some agency is clearly present, at least for those in positions of political influence.

We've already looked at the use of dog whistling to access xenophobes when anticipated stigma limits the overt expression of intolerance. The need for this tactic is obviously reduced when there are outlets of expression for the overt xenophobe. In the political arena, dog whistling is a strategy available to political candidates—and to social and political movements—to communicate with constituencies without being labeled as overt proponents of a divisive issue such as ethnically or religiously motivated opposition to immigration. It is a careful choreography in which the elite rhetoric matches masked preference (i.e., the second layer of our model). The result can be the reaping of electoral benefits—so long as the ballot is anonymous—without requiring a candidate or supporter to ever formally hold positions that invite social stigma. Dog whistling provides space for those who would prefer to avoid the overt stigma of support for a candidate, party, or movement.

Supporters of and potential voters for candidates who might invite stigmatization by overtly taking a xenophobic position walk a fine line as they try to articulate agreement with but retain a plausible distance from controversial rhetoric. The strategic goal is to have it both ways. An example of this is far-right support for certain candidates despite such candidates overtly projecting a more moderate view. Such candidates use moderation to capture a wider base while offering assurances to a more hard-line core constituency. The best indicator of a candidate's expected position is their core support rather than their words at campaign events. In France, this strategy was embraced by Marine Le Pen, who publicly presented a moderate strategy while maintaining support from traditional, more extreme constituents who accepted this type of moderation as a political necessity and theater.[6] Alternatively, candidates may embrace controversy via the overt expression of xenophobia to capture the support of voters who would not claim such positions in interactions like opinion polls. In other words, the dog whistle is very audible, but the endorsement of the candidate can be difficult to observe because it is easily masked in some interactions (e.g., telephone surveys). An example of this is the presidential politics in the United States, where Donald Trump embraced strident rhetoric about a closed border, joining in with chants about building a wall, but also received significant support from more moderate supporters from the Republican Party, at least in terms of expressed positions on migration. A two-party system with its requisite absence of options, enables this more open approach to xenophobia, which highlights the gravitation toward xenophobic elite discourse without a reduction in social stigma that might be expected in society more broadly. Rather than seeking support on less stigmatizing issues, this strategy leverages the ability of reluctant proponents of overt xenophobia to mask their opinions while still being motivated to organize. Voting is an anonymous act after all.

These examples highlight that the role of elite rhetoric in shaping the norms and strategies available to the xenophobe is far from static. Instead, the anticipation of stigma and the resultant preference for overt or covert forms of expression emerge from the interplay of key moments (e.g., campaigns, referenda, policy changes) and baseline levels of social stigma attached to overt forms of xenophobia, which can be specific to a social, political, or geographic context. In addition, elite rhetoric is a two-way street. Just as some elite expressions of overt xenophobia, like that espoused by a public figure, can normalize the role of the xenophobe and shift it toward the mainstream, elite rhetoric can also push the expectation of stigma in the other direction. In the latter case, campaigns linking overt support for issues like a border wall with targeted and more widely stigmatized flavors of xenophobia (e.g., racism) can lead to a context in which masking is more likely. In this scenario, overt expression of xenophobia by elites, when confronted with a successful alternative, can push the xenophobe further underground. Campaigns are contested spaces, and there is no single strategy that can be successful or anticipated in all contexts.

EUROPEAN POPULISM AND THE XENOPHOBE IN ELECTORAL POLITICS

Of course, populism did not invent xenophobia or create the xenophobe as a desired constituency. Simple ideological dichotomies that capture left–right orientations also distinguish cleavages on the issue of migration or, more precisely, opposition to it. Broadly, the link between a stated political orientation and antipathy toward migrants has been well established.[7] A quick summary of this left–right orientation in Europe is that those with a right or center-right orientation are relatively more opposed to migration and, in some cases, more averse to other aspects of diversity linked to migration (e.g., intermarriage, religiosity, non-Christian religious affiliation) than those oriented toward the left or center-left. The interpretation is straightforward. Political ideology reflects genuine differences in moral framing, and migration is an issue that can be clearly linked to other concepts such as human rights, freedom of movement, and tolerance of diversity to name a few. Those on the left can be framed by an inclination toward internationalism, mirrored in a greater willingness to engage with supranational entities like the European Union, and skepticism of a singular view of national demographic composition, seeing diversity as beneficial. Those on the right often fall on the opposite side of the issue, blending support for national and sociocultural continuity, which can manifest as a consolidated view of identity rooted in religion, race, or ethnicity, with a need for political and economic sovereignty linked to a clear view of defined national borders.[8]

What populism has done to these traditional cleavages, characterized by notions of what does (or does not) constitute the ideological right or left, is illuminate the role of strident rhetoric in (re)shaping norms about xenophobic expression. Returning to the multilayered model of the xenophobe, the role of populism is that of an instigator of contextual change. Any shift in expression is a strategic reaction. As a top-down catalyst—albeit with some agency—elite expression and associated support for anti-immigrant sentiment, which can be observed at the ballot box or via measures of public opinion, create shifts in the extent to which the xenophobe anticipates social stigma and might strategically choose masked expression. As we saw with the financial crisis in the United States, stigma is malleable and impermanent. The question is not if but when. *When* does a change in the stigma of overt xenophobia preclude or facilitate certain forms of xenophobic expression?

The first place to look is to the right. Although any political stripe is subject to a shift in the stigmatization of xenophobia, populist movements are notably more influential on the right. This finding does not mean that the political right, defined by ideological affiliation or party affiliation, has welcomed populism with open arms. Instead, supporters of populist movements have invited labels like "new right," "populist radical right,"[9] and "populist radical-right parties."[10] Despite some clear electoral success and encroaching influence on the broader political discussion, the tie that binds disparate populist movements in Europe is elusive. A strong contender, however, is the issue of immigration. In fact, some argue—this author included—that opposition to immigration is the only issue that can be used to consistently identify populism.[11] Other positions are notoriously inconsistent and, without using positions on migration or borders, it is unclear if the term *populist* can be coherently applied. In other policy domains, there are clear overlaps with economic and social policy that include traditional positions of the left and the right.[12] In some ways, the xenophobe is the key ingredient that makes populism, as a marker of collective action, interpretable in contemporary contexts. The xenophobe embodies a constituency that blends right-wing identification with strong antipathy toward migrants, which is the combination that some contest is the only coherent delineation between populist and conventional political options.[13]

Recently, Europe and the United States felt the social and political stirrings of a rise in overtly populist[14] political movements that—despite little in the way of shared values on many issues like social benefits or economic policy—are bound by a shared antipathy toward migration.[15] Notable political success in the Netherlands for the Party for Freedom (*Partij voor de Vrijheid*), under the leadership of the relatively popular and controversial Geert Wilders, has paralleled an increasingly prominent role for the more-established and ever-evolving National Rally (*Rassemblement National*) in France (formerly the National Front [*Front National*]). These examples are but two of many instances of increasingly influential antimigrant populist movements in most EU countries spanning contexts as distinct as Hungary, Spain, and Italy. Even Ireland, where the pattern for xenophobic political movements was unambiguously one of electoral failure, there are signs that the context is changing. Identity Ireland, a now-defunct political party that arose in 2015 and never gained a seat, highlights the historical difficulty with which xenophobic sentiment translated into electoral success. More recent movements are better at navigating the multilayered xenophobe. Ireland First, which emerged in late 2022, is pursuing an approach of intentionally masking more stigmatized political positions that might offer a more strategic pathway forward.[16] The strong tradition of a two-party system in the United States prevents independent political movements from easily operating outside the mainstream, but factions within the Republican Party, reflected in the one-term success of Donald Trump, have rallied behind strong xenophobic rhetoric like targeted bans on newcomers from Muslim-majority countries and the construction of a wall at the border between the United States and Mexico.[17] Neither objective was achieved, but the political advantage garnered from overt support for objectively xenophobic policies (i.e., targeting specific religious groups, suggesting physical barriers at some borders but not at others) clearly demonstrated the strategic benefit of such policies.

Now let's consider a perfect storm that began to brew in the late-austerity period in the United Kingdom. Before the tempest of Brexit tore through the British (or more specifically, the English) political landscape in 2015 and 2016, the features of contemporary populism began to come into focus. As the following section underscores, elites in the United Kingdom became increasingly focused on borders because migration was coupled with EU expansion. The European Union has always had a tense relationship with ethnonationalist notions of in-group identity. The process of foregrounding xenophobic rhetoric was amplified by the emergence of alternative candidates within UK politics, exemplified by the strident rhetoric of candidates like Nigel Farage. This chapter is interested in what these political machinations mean for context and the strategic options of the xenophobe in the broader society. Did all that bluster reconfigure the xenophobe's anticipation of stigma? Was there a strategic adjustment? Did people start to overtly say what they had previously masked?

BREXIT AND ELITE RHETORIC AS A CATALYST OF (IN)TOLERANCE

The United Kingdom, like the United States, recorded an uptick in interest in the issue of migration as the economy deteriorated in late 2007 and early 2008.[18] The postcrisis rise in the salience of

TABLE 4.1 KEY DATES IN THE BREXIT TIMELINE

Date	Event
January 23, 2013	David Cameron declares that a referendum should be held by 2017
July 2015	Leave.EU founded
October 8, 2015	Vote Leave founded
October 12, 2015	Britain Stronger in Europe founded
February 20, 2016	Date of referendum announced
June 23, 2016	Referendum vote held

the issue of international and EU migration belied a longer trend toward more restrictionist preferences by the UK general public since the mid-1990s.[19] Against this backdrop, an opportunity to assess the role of nonmaterial discourse also materialized. It took the form of a referendum on the continued membership of the United Kingdom in the European Union that became known as "Brexit" (a portmanteau of "British" and "exit"). Ahead of the referendum, both the pro- and anti-Brexit campaigns injected a tone and pitch to the rhetoric of migration that was helped immensely by the emergence of a political objective. This was a planned focus rather than the somewhat remote and impersonal economic cycle. Brexit and the buildup to it provide a clear-cut example of an attempt to shape public sentiment via elite rhetoric.

Before turning to the consequences of Brexit, it is helpful to understand the timeline of the campaigns for and against the United Kingdom's departure from the European Union (table 4.1). The initiation of the campaigns does not lend itself to a single date. Many consider October 8, 2015, to be the start because this date marks the formation of the organization Vote Leave,[20] which eventually became the officially designated campaign entity in favor of Brexit by the UK Electoral Commission and as such was entitled to public funding.[21] Although nearly identical in terms of timing, one could also accept a slightly earlier date in September when the influential coalition Leave.EU, which included more populist political organizations (e.g., the United Kingdom Independence Party [UKIP]). Alternatively, a later date of February 20, 2016, is also possible because it was this date that the prime minister officially announced the referendum and, moreover, allowed members of government to actively campaign. The campaign in favor of remaining in the European Union followed a similar timeline and was marked by the launch of the organization Britain Stronger in Europe on October 12, 2015—only days after the formation of Vote Leave. Similarly, this group emerged as the UK Electoral Commission's officially designated entity opposed to Brexit and as such was also entitled to matching public funding. Regardless of the date selected, by mid-October the table was set, and the elite players in the Brexit debate had emerged.

The key pillars of the Brexit debate, at least as articulated by proponents of the leave campaign, were twofold: political and sociocultural. The political issue was generally framed as an issue of border control. The points of contention targeted the discretion the United Kingdom had over EU and non-EU immigration. The latter was not a direct concern because EU member states retain discretion over immigration policy pertinent to newcomers from non-EU states; thus, the leave argument focused on the recent and potential experiences of EU enlargement. The antipathy was rooted in a perception of the experience of the somewhat recent entrance of large sending countries (e.g., Poland) to the European Union. The borders argument was fundamentally materialist and articulated in the form of a nonspecific exception to additional competition for jobs and wages.

Of note, the post-Brexit decline in the availability of labor from these same sending countries—haulage in particular—crippled the United Kingdom's short-term ability to distribute fuel.[22] In other words, there were two sides to the migration debate, but the proponents of Brexit linked a reduction in migration to a material benefit to the United Kingdom.

Sociocultural cleavages also emerged as a core delineation between those who were pro-Brexit and the opposition. This perspective coupled racialized notions of national identity with Islamophobic sentiment. The most famous manifestation of this was the strident rhetoric of Nigel Farage of UKIP, who was a ubiquitous and tireless actor in the leave campaign and the post-victory process of negotiation. A succinct example that encapsulates this strategy is the infamous campaign poster that placed the phrase "Breaking Point" over a photograph of a line of refugees taken in Slovenia in 2015 by the Getty Images photographer Jeff Mitchell. Critics of the political propaganda pointed out the notable similarity with the Nazi propaganda shown in a 2005 BBC documentary, and Dave Prentis of the public-sector union UNISON filed a formal complaint with the police arguing that the message constituted an incitement to racial hate.[23] The intention of the poster was to suggest that refugees were going to break the United Kingdom. It was the viewer who needed to imbue the message with what exactly was going to be broken, which the visual cues implied but never made explicit. Given the image selected and the style of presentation, it was a not-too-subtle dog whistle that left little doubt about the constituency it intended to energize.

Populist appeal to racially motivated xenophobes constituted a prominent component of the sociocultural appeals within the campaign in favor of Brexit, but it was not the only voice. Those opposed to leaving the European Union also focused on the pro-Brexit campaign's use of sociocultural threat, homing in on the targeting of Islamophobes and ethnocentrism. The objective was to link in the minds of the public two issues: Brexit and broader issues of intolerances rooted in religion, ethnicity, and race. In essence, the Brexit debate can be interpreted as a *competition* between countercurrents of stigma. High-profile work underlined the association between an increase in hate crime and Islamophobic discourse by political elites.[24] In other words, xenophobic discourse had plausible concrete and physical consequences. Although being xenophobic was not necessarily a prerequisite for supporting Brexit, opponents of exiting the European Union expressed relatively less anxiety over racial and religious diversity.[25] Returning to the multilayered xenophobe, the Brexit debate introduced the potential for the overt expression of intolerance to enter or be pushed further from the public sphere. Campaigns are inherently competitive. It is not just about elite rhetoric occurring in a vacuum; it is also about the reaction of the audience to the rhetoric. Either might influence the social stigma the xenophobe anticipates and by extension the strategy used to express intolerance.

Simply put, the context that Brexit fomented is one of countervailing winds. Blowing in one direction, we find elite rhetoric, which demonstrably pursued an overtly xenophobic tone. This rhetoric had the potential to directly affect the extent to which the general population could anticipate social stigma when overtly targeting migration to the United Kingdom, national control of the border, and specific reference to recent refugee migration. Theoretically, this rhetoric could have reduced the stigma associated with xenophobia by mainstreaming intolerance, which could have plausibly shaped a context in which open opposition could find a motivated and willing audience. Blowing in the opposite direction was the rhetoric of the organized opposition to Brexit, which sought to leverage the same rhetoric that threatened to mainstream intolerance. The objective was different in that opposition to Brexit sought to underscore the links to stigmatized forms of intolerance. The goal was to prevent the xenophobe from disentangling the social stigma of racial, religious, and cultural intolerance from the issues of border control. In other words, both campaigns sought to find advantage in race-based, ethnocentric, and Islamophobic rhetoric but with opposing objectives. This opposition, perhaps more than the substance of the debate itself, emerged as the core feature of the campaigns, which were characterized by dueling efforts to legitimate and discredit overtly xenophobic rhetoric. The success of one campaign or the other can be interpreted by the pattern of strategic masking observed when sentiment is expressed toward targeted groups (e.g., Muslims). In other words, it is not just about the vote but also how the Brexit campaigns changed the norms governing the expression of xenophobia after the dust had somewhat settled.

EVALUATING OVERT AND COVERT XENOPHOBIA BEFORE AND AFTER BREXIT

The evidence used here is drawn from a survey experiment that I conducted before and after the Brexit referendum vote with my colleague Amaney Jamal, some results of which were published in 2022 (see appendix 2 for a detailed overview of the experimental design).[26] The basic design used here—and throughout the book—is rooted in the experimental approach of the list experiment introduced in chapter 2. As mentioned, the key mechanism of this measure is the mitigation of social stigma by manipulating the extent to which participants are provided anonymity. In addition, in the Brexit study, independent samples were presented one of three frames that defined newcomers to the United Kingdom: Muslim, Eastern European, or Caribbean. For each frame, overt and covert support were ascertained via the selective denial or offer of absolute and permanent anonymity. Support was measured by respondents' agreement with the statement "The UK should allow people from Muslim/Eastern European/Caribbean countries to come and live here." We conducted this experiment, using these frames and the manipulation of anonymity, both before and after the Brexit referendum vote. Without repeating all the technical details provided in chapter 2, it is important to emphasize that each experimental group consisted of an independent and representative sample of the United Kingdom,[27] and as such the results are generalizable to the general public in the United Kingdom. The experiment permitted us to directly compare covert xenophobic expression with overt xenophobic expression and, most insightfully, to examine the extent to which masking occurred—before and after the referendum vote.

For a more intuitive perspective of the design, let's consider the results. Using the 2015 experiment, which constitutes the pre-Brexit sample, table 4.2 reports those who reported overt support for Muslim, Eastern European, and Caribbean immigration as a percentage of the adult population. We also knew the percentage who expressed similar sentiment but did so with the understanding that their opinions would not (and could not) be known. This was the covert expression of xenophobia. When these two percentages are compared, the result is the percentage point difference between overt and covert sentiment. If the overt sentiment is greater, which is what would be expected if the expression of intolerance incurs some degree of stigmatization, the difference would be the percentage of the population that expresses tolerance only when doing so reveals their preferences to others. Again, this result does not lead to an interpretation that anonymously expressed sentiment reflects the "true" underlying prevalence of xenophobes. This interpretation is neither theoretically nor empirically sound. As with some notorious online forums, expressing opinions anonymously can also be an opportunity to experiment with extreme posturing. Covert expression is the form of intolerance that escapes traditional polling, social media posting by identifiable users, and widespread use in public forums. It is an inner layer of the xenophobe and cannot be interpreted independently from that observed on the exterior. Again, the overt and covert occur in parallel.

Now let's see what Brexit did to the xenophobe. The results shown in table 4.2 capture shifts in the extent to which distinct layers of our model of the xenophobe were affected by contextual change. These shifts provide insight into the consequences of the heightened rhetoric—on both sides—of the Brexit referendum. The change—overall and by political preference—indicates whether the stigma of xenophobia increased or decreased because of the campaign.

The first and most glaring insight of the experiment is the substantial difference between overt and covert xenophobes. Consider the frame that presents Eastern European migrants. Before Brexit, half the estimated adult population overtly agreed that people from Eastern Europe should be able to come and live in the United Kingdom. This number, recorded at 52 percent after the vote, changed in no meaningful way. However, the gap between overt and covert expression is more of a chasm, particularly in the run-up to the vote. When offered complete and permanent anonymity, only 29 percent of the estimated adult population agreed that Eastern Europeans were welcome. This is

TABLE 4.2 SUPPORT FOR IMMIGRATION TO THE UNITED KINGDOM FROM MUSLIM-MAJORITY, EASTERN EUROPEAN, OR CARIBBEAN COUNTRIES, PRE-BREXIT AND POST-BREXIT, BY POLITICAL ORIENTATION (LEFT, CENTER, AND RIGHT)

	Percentage who agree				Percentage who mask	
	Overt		Covert		Overt–covert	
	Pre-Brexit	Post-Brexit	Pre-Brexit	Post-Brexit	Pre-Brexit	Post-Brexit
	2015	2016	2015	2016	2015	2016
Muslim-majority countries						
Overall	46%*	52%*	43%*	37%*	3%	15%*
Left	63%*	66%*	53%*	58%*	10%	8%
Center	53%*	52%*	44%*	32%*	9%	20%*
Right	37%*	42%*	18%*	17%*	19%	25%*
Eastern European countries						
Overall	50%*	52%*	29%*	37%*	21%*	15%*
Left	66%*	66%*	41%*	63%*	25%*	3%
Center	48%*	51%*	19%*	18%*	29%*	33%*
Right	40%*	43%*	30%*	34%*	10%	9%
Caribbean countries						
Overall	57%*	62%*	37%*	46%*	20%*	16%*
Left	70%*	74%*	33%*	79%*	37%*	–5%
Center	57%*	61%*	48%*	38%*	9%	23%*
Right	47%*	55%*	25%*	33%*	22%*	22%*

Source: University of Essex, Institute for Social and Economic Research Innovation Panel Wave 8, 2015; Innovation Panel Wave 9, 2016, Understanding Society: Innovation Panel, Wave 8, 2015; NatCen Social Research 2015, 2016.

Note: The overt question was worded as follows: "Do you think the UK should allow people from Muslim/Eastern European/Caribbean countries to come and live here?" The covert question was worded similarly but administered such that no direct indication of support or opposition was required. (See chapter 2 for a more detailed description of the technique and appendix 2 for the full text of all questions.) In the table, * indicates that the reported percentage is significantly different from zero (p ≤ 0.10).

a highly significant and substantive difference of 21 percentage points. In other words, an estimated one-fifth of adults revealed support for Eastern European migrants only when their opinion was revealed. The post-Brexit difference, at 15 percentage points, was less, which will be discussed in more detail in a moment. Caribbean migrants confront a context of reception similar to that of Eastern Europeans. Before Brexit, overt support was reported at 57 percent and climbed slightly higher after the Brexit vote, reaching 62 percent. Covert sentiment was notably less welcoming. Only 37 percent agreed that Caribbean migrants should be permitted to arrive before Brexit, which climbed to 46 percent after the vote. At 20 percentage points before Brexit and 16 percentage points after, the percentage of the population masking their intolerance for Caribbean migrants is notably similar to that observed for Eastern European migrants.

Muslims, however, confronted something quite different. Before Brexit, overt support for migrants from Muslim-majority countries (46 percent) was less than that shown for Eastern European and Caribbean newcomers, although not by much. In other words, the overt xenophobe seemed to distinguish little among the three frames used in this experiment. Covert expression tells a very different story. Where the Eastern Europe and Caribbean frames recorded drops in support of migration of 21 percentage points and 20 percentage points, respectively, when anonymity was provided, the difference between overt and covert support for Muslims was only 3 percentage points. To the extent to which formal tests of difference are useful, this level of masking does not even approach significance. Put another way, there was little discernible stigma to being an overt Islamophobe. Compared with the other two flavors of intolerance, opposing Muslim newcomers was not really a multilayered affair. As a side note, this pattern is not unique to the United Kingdom. Similar research, also done with Amaney Jamal, on citizenship using a comparable design found that support for Muslims being naturalized was not significantly or substantively masked in the United States.[28]

The evidence is clear: Muslim migrants are an open target and enjoy little benefit from the social stigma that mitigates overt xenophobic expression directed at Eastern European and Caribbean migrants. Be that as it may, we've learned that the context of expression is far from static. The post-Brexit period is a case in point. The difference between overt and covert sentiment increased sharply by 15 percentage points following Brexit, which is nearly identical to the result found for the other two frames. In short, the post-Brexit period shows notably similar levels of masking of xenophobic sentiment directed at Muslim, Eastern European, and Caribbean newcomers. The pre-Brexit period did not. Something changed.

What does this pattern tell us about elites and the xenophobe's adaptation to distinct social climates? First, the norms that allow people to anticipate and calibrate their expression of support can change rapidly and did so in response to the Brexit campaigns. This finding is evidenced by the percentage who were supportive of immigration to the United Kingdom only under conditions of anonymity. For all groups, the post-Brexit estimated percentage of the UK population who stated their support for migration only when asked overtly was 15 to 16 percentage points higher than before Brexit. This was a notable shift in the strategy of xenophobic expression and was directed at newcomers from Muslim-majority countries. Before Brexit, there was no evidence of social stigma affecting how support for Muslim migrants manifested— the xenophobe made no clear distinction between overt and covert expression. Clearly, the Brexit campaigns changed how social stigma was anticipated, and the respondents' stated political orientations help explain why.

For attitudes toward Muslim migrants, those at the center and right of the political spectrum found the post-Brexit landscape to be less accepting of overt xenophobia. Support held steady or increased slightly when views were expressed without the cover of anonymity. However, with anonymity, antipathy notably increased—as reflected in significantly less expressed support. The left showed little change. The overtly anti-Muslim rhetoric of the pro-Brexit campaign did not create a public forum for xenophobia. Rather than some normalization process, the campaign restricted an increasingly hardened constituency of xenophobes in the center and on the right of the political spectrum into the second layer of the multilayered model of xenophobic expression. This layer represents the intentionally and consciously masked xenophobe. An overtly xenophobic agenda by political elites can be successfully stigmatized by the opposition. The result is a shift away from the public gaze—and intentionally so.

The center and left of the political spectrum appeared to be more directly affected by elite rhetoric. The anchor of political ideology and the pull toward positions that match expectations is less strong among those who avoid the poles. For example, those who identified with the center after Brexit recorded a drop of 10 percentage points in covert support for migrants from Caribbean countries, but overt support remained nearly unchanged. Such a drop was not observed for Eastern European migrants, but covert support was already notably low before Brexit at 19 percent. The left-leaning respondents shifted in a different way. For Caribbean and Eastern European migrants, the left was less willing to state greater support after Brexit. Rather than that shift reflecting a decline in overall support, there is near stability in overt sentiment (even a slight increase for some frames) among those who identified with the left. What changed was that overt sentiment softened, and the difference between overt and covert sentiment was reduced—and notably so. This finding is attributable to two simultaneous processes. First, the left became increasingly strident about being open to immigration, which is a position that the rhetoric of Brexit brought to the fore. If one found Brexit problematic—a position put forward by most or all parties on the left—there would be little room for masked intolerance. The result was an actual increase in covert support and a convergence of the first and second layers of the multilayered model of xenophobic expression. Another process was the abandonment of the left as a political marker in the post-Brexit context. In other words, those who masked their intolerance found a more consistent home in the center or on the right. This is more of a political shift than a shift in expression and helps explain some of the increased strategic masking outside the left after Brexit.

Students of electoral behavior will surely parse the nuanced pathways by which public sentiment and political identification shifted because of the Brexit campaigns, but that is not a primary concern here. What is more important is to understand how something like Brexit can dramatically change the norms that govern the stigma of xenophobia. Targeted intolerance can be both more prevalent and increasingly hidden as a result of a campaign that puts it front and center. An understanding of the shifting role of stigma in shaping the strategy of xenophobic expression toward migrants is limited when overt sentiment alone is used to capture the context of reception. Brexit provides a window into the role of elite rhetoric more broadly, which is shown to have a complex relationship with the xenophobe. Overt intolerance from the top down can push like-minded individuals underground. It would not be strange to find an overt landscape that is highly motivated by xenophobia but that intentionally limits the extent to which intolerance is acknowledged. In other words, like the excuse that materialist logics provide, the xenophobe navigates shifting social norms by supporting and denying xenophobia at the same time. It is not about what a person thinks in some absolute sense. That is not a useful understanding of the xenophobe. It is about understanding which moments and contexts are conducive and strategically coherent for the xenophobe. There can clearly be rapid changes and opportunities for divergence between expression and behavior (e.g., voting).

THE VIEW FROM ABOVE: ELITE IMPACT ON SOCIAL STIGMA AND THE POLITICAL MAINSTREAM

This chapter and the previous one underline the materialist and political factors that have driven recent patterns of xenophobic expression in the United States and Europe. Both are essentially top-down mechanisms, although there is far greater intention in the targeted elite rhetoric. The rise of populist parties in both contexts, linked by antipathy toward migration and migrants and support for national control of borders, reveals the paradox of the contemporary xenophobe. Changes in context (e.g., economic crises, strident political campaign rhetoric) shape how the stigma of intolerance is anticipated. This shift leads to changes in the strategy by which the xenophobe navigates the public and private arenas, which is a view quite different from one that sees the xenophobe as a fixed and observable social actor. Instead, the xenophobe is multilayered—clearly a theme here—and that means that mainstream expressions of intolerance are only partially informative—also a consistent theme.

Succinctly put, outside forces substantially alter our anticipation of how xenophobia will be interpreted. In the United States, material concerns provide a way to present intolerance that avoids leaning on racist or religious bigotry. This finding does not mean that racism or religious intolerance are not present or that they do not motivate the xenophobe. Instead, materialist concerns offer a less stigmatized logic and therefore a route by which the xenophobe can access the mainstream. Elites offer a similar pathway: the polarization of a contentious campaign like that in favor of Brexit created a very different context for the xenophobe from that of the financial crisis in the United States. Rather than a broadly shared concern, like economic precarity, the Brexit campaigns used migration as a cleavage to differentiate support for and opposition to European integration, or borders more broadly. In this case, elite rhetoric provided the opportunity for xenophobes to coalesce around an issue. Unlike the economic context, the Brexit campaigns were a less consolidated experience. A bitterly divided sociopolitical context resulted in increased strategic masking as the two campaigns sought to use the xenophobe to their advantage. The xenophobe might have been motivated to politically engage, increasingly feeling a sense of antipathy toward migrants and, at the same time, to anticipate greater stigma.

If there is a single takeaway from the case studies presented in this chapter and the previous one, it is the following: stigma hates consensus. The broader the acceptance of an argument against migration, the less stigmatized the expression of xenophobia becomes. The more divided or controversial an anti-immigrant position becomes, the greater the pressure to strategically mask.

III

RACE, RELIGION, AND REFUGEES

The Expression of Targeted Intolerance

5

COLOR-BLIND OR
INTENTIONALLY LOOKING AWAY?

(UN)INTENTIONALITY: CONSCIOUS AND
UNCONSCIOUS LAYERS OF XENOPHOBIA,
RACISM, AND ETHNOCENTRISM

Recent scholarship underlines the disconnect between what we say and what we do, particularly on the issues of race and ethnicity.[1] When people are asked directly, they often decisively deny any prejudices based on characteristics like race or ethnicity—or most observable attributes for that matter. However, differences in many key societal outcomes (e.g., hiring, earnings, health) clearly disadvantage some groups more than others, resulting in a pattern of marginalization that, given overt denials of discriminatory attitudes, would seem to be implausible.[2] This contradiction results in a need to understand why an overt articulation of neutrality or a flat-out denial of prejudicial attitudes does not seem to convert into equitable outcomes in other domains.

To better understand the processes by which overt attitudes and behavior diverge, work on the perpetuation of marginalization has shifted from a focus on overt expressions of intolerance, racial or otherwise, toward mechanisms that are seemingly masked even from the potentially biased individual. The result is an interesting and clear documentation of unconscious forms of bias.[3] From this perspective, the maintenance of discriminatory behaviors results from the existence of unspoken and unobserved pathways that facilitate an individual's ability to both deny and act upon biases in parallel.[4] The key insight is the simultaneous denial and perpetuation of intolerant perspectives that support theoretical models of racism in which the individual is unaware of the existence of intrinsic biases.[5] A manifestation of this self-denial is a color-blind narrative and a bifurcation of intolerance into two reservoirs: one outspoken and the other masked from all, even those who perpetuate it.

Unconscious biases do not cancel out overt expressions of intolerance. It is worth reiterating that overt prejudice—whether it be racism, ethnocentrism, or something else—remains an observed part of social interaction. No acknowledgment of the disingenuity of the color-blind narrative diminishes the impact and reality of overt forms of racial and ethnic prejudice. As the previous chapters have reinforced, xenophobic expression can be (and often is) overtly expressed. This assertion is backed by a large interdisciplinary body of research that underlines the impact of overt forms of discrimination, particularly by race.[6] More to the point, open expressions of intolerance, like those expressed at the 2017 "Unite the Right" rally in Charlottesville, Virginia,[7] and the large rallies by Patriotic Europeans Against the Islamisation of the West (PEGIDA) in Germany in late-2014 and early 2015,[8] remain salient attributes of public social interaction. In short, unconscious and very-much-conscious forms of bigotry continue to coexist, and the intention of this chapter is to advance our understanding of masked intolerance but not at the cost of understating the impact of overt, public, and revealed prejudicial attitudes and behaviors.

What does all this have to do with the xenophobe? As pointed out in the introduction, the xenophobe is best understood as a general manifestation of many forms of intolerance. The multi-layered model of xenophobic expression highlights the need to define a theoretical, and sometimes purely hypothetical, "other" toward which opposition can be directed, thus reducing racism and ethnocentrism to merely xenophobic flavors. Instead, the model reveals a mechanism by which intolerances manifest—whether directed exclusively at newcomers or as part of broader prejudicial practices—and underscores that overt and unconscious forms of bias are not the only two options of xenophobic expression. Racial and ethnic intolerance can emerge from a third layer that, like unconscious biases, does not lend itself well to direct observation. However, unlike unconscious biases, the mechanism by which this reservoir of intolerance is concealed involves some degree of volition, and as a result the key mechanism is *intentionality*.

STIGMA, RACE, AND MOTIVES FOR CONCEALMENT

Why might the xenophobe conceal attitudes rooted in racial or ethnic prejudice differently from those targeting other dimensions? The simple answer is that these concepts are far from independent. Theoretically, given the role of stigmatization in shaping expression, the xenophobe is responsive to the link between the overt expression of opposition toward migrants (i.e., antipathy toward the generalized newcomer) and racially or ethnically motivated forms of intolerance. This link is important because it prevents a discussion of xenophobia from focusing exclusively on the migrant as a unidimensional other. Because this view of the migrant is unlikely to hold (expect perhaps in moments of economic crisis, as described in chapter 3), attitudes toward migrants are never fully decoupled from other forms of identity that intersect

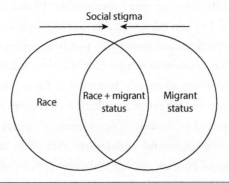

FIGURE 5.1 Social stigma and the intersection of race and migrant status

with attributes like race, ethnicity, and religion. As such, the stigma that goes along with expressing overtly racist sentiment cannot be decoupled from that anticipated for overt expressions of opposition to migrants or migration more broadly (figure 5.1).

Theoretically, linking race or ethnicity as a core attribute of migrants *also* creates a link between different types of social stigma. The extent to which this connection is anticipated can result in the xenophobe choosing covert instead of overt expression. This view is different from one suggesting that the racialization of migration leads to a reduction in xenophobia. This view requires that subsequent to a link being made, the xenophobe must find the expression of intolerance to be unappealing regardless of the layers of expression available. Without a clear accounting of intentional masking, whether a change of heart has occurred is speculative. Just because less racially motivated intolerance is observed does not mean that all layers of xenophobic expression are equally affected. Why? Because we know that the presence of social stigma can result in a reduction in the prevalence of overt xenophobia. In addition, the inclusion of a perception that racism and xenophobia are intertwined theoretically increases the expectation of stigmatization and, similarly, the likelihood that intentional masking is the preferred strategy of xenophobic expression. In short, a social context in which more stigma is attached to racism or ethnocentrism than to other attributes is also a context in which there is a greater incentive to mask intolerance.

To offer a hypothetical contextual example, consider a simple comparison that highlights the strategic calculus of race-based xenophobic expression. Overt opposition to migration might plausibly be decoupled from racial preferences and, with the help of contextual factors like economic precarity or elite rhetoric, emerge with little anticipation of stigma. However, in the same contexts, when asking about preferences toward migrant groups that highlight racial attributes—whether it be by country of origin or explicitly defining the race of the newcomer—the same respondents are likely to anticipate social stigma and to intentionally reconsider overtly expressing xenophobic preferences. Alternatively, making a link between opposition to migrants and race-based preferences could result in an actual change of heart at all levels. Distinguishing these two outcomes is a key insight of a multilayered perspective.

NORMATIVE TOLERANCE, HISTORICAL EMIGRATION, AND RACIALIZED XENOPHOBIA: IN-GROUP PREFERENCES IN THE NETHERLANDS AND IRELAND

Now let's move to evidence. We'll consider two contexts—the Netherlands and Ireland—to highlight the links between racial or ethnic preferences and the xenophobe. In both cases—as with every example in the book—I've used a survey experiment to vary the extent to which individuals could be assured of permanent and absolute anonymity when expressing their opinions about migrants (see chapter 2 for a detailed introduction to the technique). Before presenting the results, some specifics of these two survey experiments deserve mention.

First, the Netherlands is a context in which the divergence between overt and covert expressions of sentiment is of increasingly obvious concern. Specifically, in recent memory, political polls have poorly tracked public opinion on the issue of migration. At the same time, the same issue figures prominently in the political arena. In other words, there is a disconnect between an anonymous outcome (i.e., a vote) and overtly expressed sentiment (i.e., public opinion), which suggests that the role of stigma is relevant to the context and that masking is a likely strategy of expression. To give a brief overview, let's consider the case of the Party for Freedom (*Partij voor de Vrijheid* [PVV]). The PVV and its controversial leader, Geert Wilders, reflected a strong populist and antimigrant voice in Dutch politics until 2019—and perhaps beyond.[9] What stands out is the overtly tolerant position toward immigrants taken by most of the public in the Netherlands, which is hard to reconcile with the support for hard-line, restrictive positions represented by the PVV. In 2016, the party's vote total was rising, but just over one-third directed overt antipathy toward Muslim migrants. In contrast, more than two-thirds of the public in Greece, Italy, Poland, and Hungary viewed Muslims negatively at the time.[10] Moreover, Wilders was tried and convicted for public statements targeting specific immigrant groups but acquitted of related charges of inciting discrimination and hate speech.[11] In short, the legal system and the social context of the Netherlands diverge notably from its electoral behavior. Voting, it should be noted, is an anonymous act. Reconciling these parallel patterns requires a more layered view of society.

Some work in the Netherlands has hinted at a divergence in opinion either in attitudes toward minority groups or migrants, which we'll build upon here.[12] Let's turn again to a survey experiment that revealed variation in the overt and covert expression of support for migrants of the same or a different race or ethnicity from that of most of the country's population. As with all experiments in this book, the respondents were selected at random, and the sample was representative of the general adult population. In this case, the experiment formed part of a larger panel called the Longitudinal Internet Studies for the Social Sciences, administered in September 2014 by the nonprofit research institute Centerdata (located at Tilburg University in the Netherlands).[13] The basic design mirrored that of the experiments conducted in the United States (chapter 3) and the United Kingdom (chapter 4). Respondents were asked about their preferences by way of two parallel methods. The first presented a direct question that captured overt sentiment. The other used the list experiment (see chapter 2) and provided absolute and permanent anonymity, thus capturing covert sentiment. The use of these methods allowed us to compare overt with covert preferences for immigrants to the Netherlands who were framed as either having the same race or ethnicity as most Dutch people or having a different race or ethnicity. Some results from this experiment were published in 2019 (in collaboration with my colleagues Philip Brenner, Peter Schmidt, and Diana Zavala-Rojas) and 2020 (see appendix 3 for a detailed overview of the experimental design).[14]

The second case we'll consider is Ireland, which deserves our attention for very different reasons from those for our observation of the Netherlands. Instead of offering insight into the disconnection between overtly expressed sentiment and political behavior, Ireland's case is rooted in the social stigma of historical memory. Specifically, the perception of migration in Ireland is intimately linked to a long history of Irish emigration.[15] In brief, the logic is as follows. Xenophobic sentiment in Ireland confronts a dimension of national identity in which Ireland has been a net contributor to global migration for a significant period of its history—both before and after it achieved independence from the United Kingdom. In addition, in some contexts of reception, Irish migrants were racialized in ways that had substantive implications for their social and economic mobility.[16]

Layered onto this history is a more recent (and somewhat unprecedented) experience of immigration to Ireland, interrupted by a brief return to net emigration after the financial crisis of 2007–2008.[17] The story is typically framed in terms material opportunism,[18] with the "Celtic Tiger" roaring in the 1990s and early 2000s, spurring return migrants of Irish nativity and newcomers from elsewhere to seek opportunities in Ireland.[19] The experience was a change from earlier patterns of net negative migration, which saw Ireland's population peak in the mid-nineteenth century[20] and in terms of the racial and ethnic homogeneity that characterized return migrants of Irish descent.[21] Ireland found itself simultaneously experiencing notable return migration and immigration from other EU countries, with nearly three-quarters of newcomers hailing from elsewhere in the European Union. Ireland was also faced with newfound diversity owing to a notably different mixture of non-EU sending countries from what the country had previously experienced. The result was the availability of two plausible mechanisms for shaping how the xenophobe in Ireland might have understood the stigma of articulating racialized oppositional sentiment: historical memory and contemporary diversity.

As with the Netherlands, the survey experiment in Ireland considered the race of the newcomer, but, in contrast to the method used in the Netherlands, the approach required participants to reference their own identity. As with all list experiments, the basic design manipulated the extent to which anonymity was available to participants. The survey experiment formed part of a nationally representative panel of the Irish adult population called the Economic Sentiment Monitor, which entered and exited the field in June 2017. The design was intentionally straightforward. The direct question queried support for "more Black people coming to live in Ireland." The explicit link with race served the purpose of inviting a degree of hesitancy in participants' responses owing to the clear, somewhat blunt, connection to the stigma of racism. As a result, it was hypothesized that overt sentiment would differ substantially from that directed at the same highly racialized frame but expressed with complete assurance of anonymity. This experiment was fielded with Frances McGinnity and Éamonn Fahey in partnership with the Irish Human Rights and Equality Commission, and some of the results were published in 2020 and 2022 (see appendix 3 for a detailed overview of the experimental design).[22]

What did these two list experiments show? Despite presenting distinct frames for race or ethnicity, both revealed that a notably stable percentage of respondents were overtly supportive of migrants when race or ethnicity was defined. This stability remained clear regardless of whether race or ethnicity was framed as shared, as different, or using a fixed definition (i.e., Black). An estimated two-thirds of the the population of the Netherlands stated that migrants, defined as having the same race or ethnicity as most Dutch people or having a different race or ethnicity, should be allowed to come to the Netherlands. Similarly, an estimated two-thirds of the Irish population reported supporting the arrival of Black newcomers. In both contexts, the overt expression of xenophobia was limited to an estimated one-third of the population, with the overwhelming majority expressing no open opposition to the arrival of racially framed migrants.

If we imagine that the xenophobe conceals nothing, the overt pattern revealed in these experiments suggests that the race or ethnicity of the newcomer matters little. The respondents in the Netherlands and Ireland seemed to express about the same level of support for newcomers regardless of race, indicated by the absence of significant or substantive variation linked to how the migrant was framed emerged. This finding does not mean that race or ethnicity does not matter. As mentioned, an estimated one-third of the adult population in each context expressed no support for the arrival of newcomers defined by race or ethnicity. What the lack of variation shows is how easily the xenophobe can be misinterpreted. It is only when anonymity is provided that notable variation emerges.

Let's start with Ireland. The second column in table 5.1 reveals the estimated percentage of the general population who overtly expressed support for Black migrants (64 percent), and the fourth column provides the percentage of those who expressed support when anonymity was guaranteed (46 percent). The percentage-point difference between the two is notably large. With anonymity, nearly an estimated two-thirds of the population who indicated overt support for Black migrants dropped by 18 percent. That is a substantive and significant decline. To generalize from this pattern, the results indicate that less than half the general population were supportive when the social stigma of expressing tolerance was mitigated. Ireland is not alone in this. In the Netherlands, when anonymity was provided, the change nearly mirrored that seen in Ireland. The decline in support was estimated at about 22 percentage points (from 62 percent to 40 percent).

TABLE 5.1 OVERT AND COVERT SUPPORT FOR MIGRANTS FRAMED BY RACE OR ETHNICITY IN IRELAND AND THE NETHERLANDS

	Percentage who support migrants				Percentage who mask
	Overt	Participants	Covert	Participants	Overt–covert
Ireland					
Black	64%*	407	46%*	404	18%*
The Netherlands					
Same race or ethnic group	62%*	699	18%*	701	43%*
Different race or ethnic group	62%*	704	40%*	698	22%*

Source: M. Creighton, L. Lilleoja, P. Schmidt, and D. Zavala-Rojas, CentERdata, LISS panel - List experiment on social desirability bias in attitudes towards immigration. DANS 2019. https://doi .org/10.17026/dans-zw3-btmr; M. J. Creighton, É. Fahey, and F. McGinnity, "Immigration, Identity, and Anonymity: Intentionally Masked Intolerance in Ireland," International Migration Review 56, no. 3 (2022): 881–910. https://doi.org/10.1177/01979183211054806.

Note: The overt questions were worded as follows: for Ireland, "Would you support more Black people coming to live in Ireland?"; for the Netherlands, "Do you think the Netherlands should allow people of the same race or ethnic group as most Dutch people to come and live here?" and "Do you think the Netherlands should allow people of a different race or ethnic group from most Dutch people to come and live here?" The covert question was worded similarly but administered such that no direct indication of support or opposition was required. (See chapter 2 for a more detailed description of the technique and appendix 3 for the full text of all questions.) In the table, * indicates that the reported percentage is significantly different from zero (p ≥ 0.05).

In both cases, covert sentiment indicated substantively and significantly lower levels of support. And in both cases, what appeared to be a clear, overt majority in support of migrants defined by race was shown to be a minority position among covert xenophobes. Again, as in the cases of the United States and the United Kingdom, this pattern reinforces the necessity of measuring strategic masking as a crucial outlet for and reservoir of xenophobic expression.

In both contexts, social stigma plainly limited the expression of xenophobic sentiment when directed at Black migrants, in the case of Ireland, and when directed at migrants of a race or ethnic group different from that of most Dutch people, in the case of the Netherlands. The second layer of the xenophobe is demonstrably more rigid in its opposition and notably strategic in its revelation of this antipathy. It is easy to see how a normative context of tolerance can radically change our view of the xenophobe, particularly when antipathy toward the other is linked to race. However, in one important way, the covert pattern remains similar to the overt pattern on these two frames (i.e., Black and racially or ethnically different migrants). Both types of expression indicate that there is a notable consistency in the overall level of support. However, when we turn our attention to attitudes toward racially similar migrants, which was measured only in the Netherlands, the narrative once again changes.

The European Social Survey, a long-running social survey of attitudes that I had the pleasure of coordinating in Ireland for several rounds, has asked a question about attitudes toward migrants of the "same race" as the majority of the population in a given country for nearly two decades. This question was designed to be contrasted with a nearly identical question worded to assess attitudes toward migrants of a "different race." In the cases of Ireland and the Netherlands, the gap between overt and covert expression of support for Black migrants or newcomers of a different race or ethnicity was about 20 percentage points. However, for the question about migrants of the same race, the gap was about double at 43 percentage points. This is a notably large difference and offers insight into how social stigma operates in the expression of intolerance. Specifically, when a racial in-group identity overlaps, the stigma of overt opposition to migration is notably higher. It is easier to express opposition if the group to which antipathy is directed is not framed as racially or ethnically distinct. However, there are clear limits to the in-group overlap in that the experiments discussed here referred to migrants not of any clear shared heritage with respondents. In other words, the racial overlap was decoupled from an in-group overlap with the identity of migrant. To consider migrant in-group dynamics linked to a diverse population of reception, let's turn to the United States.

ETHNICITY, MIGRANT BACKGROUND, AND IN-GROUP PREFERENCES AND THE UNITED STATES

Chapter 3 considered the role of materialist narratives in masking xenophobic sentiment in the United States, underscoring the surface-level nature of intolerance before the financial crisis and the role of economic forces in shaping strategies of xenophobic expression. The survey experiment discussed in chapter 3 also recorded details about the race or ethnicity of respondents, which created an opportunity to assess how one's own group membership shapes xenophobic expression.[23] Differences between self-ascribed race or ethnicity can be contrasted to reveal variation in the extent to which intolerance is overtly expressed or strategically masked. Some have found that the race and ethnicity of the survey taker also translates into variation in the difference between overt and covert expressions of intolerance,[24] although this finding is generally seen as a concern for the measurement of attitudes rather than an insight into a multilayered reality, which is the view taken here. Unlike the experiments carried out in Ireland and the Netherlands, the perspective offered by the U.S. data collection moves beyond assumptions of homogeneity, acknowledging the reality that contexts of reception are diverse. This view permits us to know the degree to which members of the population of reception are motivated by in-group and out-group preferences.

The largest source of migrants to the United States is Latin America. Although not a coherent label of self-identification in many contexts of origin, migrants of Latin American origin in the United States can (and often do) coalesce around the term *Hispanic*. In 2018, Hispanic-identifying members of the general population numbered just under sixty million, about one-third (about twenty million) of whom were born outside the United States.[25] Aside from those who identify as White alone (about two hundred million), Hispanic is the largest ethnic group in the United States, surpassing Blacks and Asians.[26] As has been pointed out,[27] Latin American migrants are a large and salient component of migration to the United States overall and as such the nonimmigrant Hispanic population in the United States plausibly perceives this ethnicity to be an in-group identity of meaning. Moreover, it is a shared construct between migrant and nonmigrant self-identifying Hispanics.

In addition to the link between Hispanic self-identification and migration, the term *border* in the United States is closely associated with that separating the United States from Mexico. When xenophobic messaging is used for political gain, as in the case of the 2016 presidential election, the chant "Build the wall" did not require clarification that there would be no construction of such a wall at the northern border with Canada. This contextual reality (i.e., the link between ethnicity and migration and an emphasis on the southern border of the United States) informed the framing operationalized in the U.S. list experiment, which queried support for a closed border. The frame intentionally avoided an explicitly racial or ethnic link in the wording of the target of

TABLE 5.2 OVERT AND COVERT SUPPORT FOR A CLOSED BORDER IN THE UNITED STATES BY RACE OR ETHNICITY

	Percentage who oppose a closed border				Percentage who mask
	Overt	Participants	Covert	Participants	Overt–covert
Hispanic respondents	51%*	84	55%*	84	–3%
Black respondents	30%*	74	13%*	149	17%*
White respondents	43%*	575	28%*	1,169	15%*

Source: Mathew J. Creighton and Amaney A. Jamal, "Perceptions of Islam, Migration and Citizenship in the United States: A List Experiment," Time-Sharing Experiments for the Social Sciences, 2010, https://www.tessexperiments.org/study/creighton022.

Note: The overt question was worded as follows: "Do you support or oppose cutting off all immigration to the United States?" The covert question was worded similarly but administered such that no direct indication of support or opposition was required. (See chapter 2 for a more detailed description of the technique and appendix 1 for the full text of all questions.) In the table, * indicates that the reported percentage is significantly different from zero (p ≥ 0.05).

support or opposition, as was the case in the experiments conducted in Ireland and the Netherlands. The reference was to the border instead. The resulting data allowed us to consider variation in terms of the racial or ethnic self-identification of the respondents as directed toward migration with no clear racial or ethnic composition specified. Some results from these data were published with my colleague Alessandra Bazo Vienrich in 2018 (see appendix 1 for a detailed overview of the experimental design).[28]

Table 5.2 reveals the pattern of expression by the racial or ethnic self-identification of respondents. The second column provides the percentage of respondents who overtly expressed opposition to a closed border. The only group within which a majority overtly opposed closing the border—and just barely at that—was Hispanic respondents at 51 percent. The gap in overt opposition was notable between Hispanic and Black respondents at about 20 percent. White respondents reported somewhat greater opposition to a closed border than Black respondents at 43 percent, but a clear gap was also found between Hispanic and White respondents, in this case at around 8 percent.

The percentages of covert expression of opposition to a closed border show a clear pattern of masking among Black and White respondents but not among Hispanic respondents. The percentage of Black respondents opposing a closed border declined by more than half to 13 percent. Similarly, albeit with a slightly less steep decline, White respondents reported notably less opposition when expressing covert sentiment—declining from 43 percent to 28 percent. In stark contrast, Hispanic respondents reported nearly identical covert opposition to a closed border relative to that expressed overtly. This finding reflects the very different strategic responses to the issue of migration in the U.S. context.

Clearly, something interesting happens in terms of the social stigma attached to being a xenophobe when it overlaps with a Hispanic identity. While a different posture may be offered when one is able to strategically mask one's preferences, the approach of appearing tolerant remains a salient strategy for White and Black respondents in a way that is not shared with Hispanic respondents. One interpretation, shared by me, is that in-group identity changes how the stigmatization of anti-immigrant sentiment is anticipated. In the cases of Ireland and the Netherlands (see table 5.1), the framing was intentionally presented such that race was an essential and inextricable attribute of the migrant. Respondents were forced to link an overt expression of intolerance with a racial or ethnic motive. Even when the question was self-referential, as in the case of the Netherlands (where respondents were asked about migrants of the same or a different race or ethnic group from that of most Dutch people), the focus remained squarely on a defined race or ethnicity of the migrant. In the case of the experiment in the United States (see table 5.2), the intersection was between the respondent's own race or ethnicity and a general perception of migration restrictionism. That link, however, was not so easily avoided for Hispanic respondents.

The U.S. results indicate that if a shared in-group identity intersects with *two* dimensions of xenophobia—in this case, race or ethnicity and migrant status—the result is a decline (or elimination) of masking—so long as race is not defined as an explicit dimension of the migrant. This is the case because the covert xenophobe is not a relevant actor in the Hispanic population because the covert xenophobe does not share the strategic advantage of masking available to Black and White people. The United States is a useful context within which to observe this intersection because Hispanics, both those born in the United States and those born elsewhere, constitute a large community and have a distinct relationship with contemporary migration flows. If the framing of the question had paralleled that of the Netherlands in that the race of the newcomers had been compared to that of the context of destination, some masking caused by overstated overt tolerance might emerge—as it did in Ireland and the Netherlands. However, when the role of race or ethnicity is not explicitly linked to the overt expression of xenophobia, masking does not result. Instead, in-group identity leads to a clear expression of tolerance that is stable, even when absolute and permanent anonymity is provided.

THE PARADOX OF COVERT ACTS AND OVERT EXPRESSION

The final point to raise in this discussion is about the societal implications of intentionally masked racial and ethnic xenophobia. Why is it insightful to understand when covert expression is intentional? Both intentional and unintentional covert expression are distinct from overt expression and as such are not clearly in need of conceptual distinction. That said, they have very different societal implications, which can be linked to overt and covert *acts*. What a clear understanding of intentionality offers is a view of the xenophobe that, when overt expression skews tolerant, does not attribute the continued presence of xenophobia to an unconscious phenomenon. Being color-blind is more of a strategy than an actual state of mind. It is not a rejection of the idea that racism can be color-blind in its articulation. The evidence for this is clear,[29] and unconscious manifestations of intolerance play an important role in the perpetuation of xenophobia. But the observed and theoretical importance of intentionality highlights the existence of preferences that are deliberately relegated to interactions in which concerns about social stigma can be alleviated (e.g., in situations of anonymity). Such situations return agency to the xenophobe; thus, we should question interventions that assume that unexpressed intolerance is only a by-product of the unintentional, unconscious, or unknown.

Let's start with overtly xenophobic acts. It remains true that, even in normatively tolerant contexts (e.g., Ireland, the Netherlands), some intolerant interactions remain overt in nature. In the case of the United States, overtly intolerant social norms, including those codified in law (e.g., prohibitions again interracial marriage; segregated transportation, hospitality, and schools), are not too far in the past. Whether it be Jim Crow laws or migration policy that reflects ethnocentric preferences, overtly defined biases are not unheard of or, in some cases, even uncommon. However, when norms shift toward an expectation of equity in treatment or neutrality in terms of race or ethnicity, the xenophobe confronts social stigma that increases the cost of overtly xenophobic behavior. This is not to say that all xenophobic acts would be sanctioned everywhere by everyone. This point simply underscores the expectation that the xenophobe would *act* strategically, just as we observed xenophobic expression to be selectively presented in this chapter—particularly when race or ethnicity and migrant identity overlap. The key point here is that the norms leading to the stigmatization of the overt xenophobe can really be expected to affect only overt acts. Covert acts are another matter.

Of course, covert xenophobic acts do not necessarily require intentionality, but it certainly can play a role. Just as expressed xenophobia can be substantially greater when permanent anonymity is provided, acts that avoid public scrutiny easily perpetuate race-based or ethnocentric intolerances. Examples include voting, hiring, social bonding (e.g., friendship, partnership), residential choice, and school preference. These situations do not require any overt acknowledgment of a decision being motivated by intolerance. To be certain, an overlap with unconscious preferences is present. One might not acknowledge, even to oneself, why a choice of housing or partner is preferable, but this choice could be linked to latent racial or ethnic preferences. In fact, in all likelihood, a direct query would result in a denial of any link with intolerances rooted in race or ethnicity or with migrant background—a pattern akin to that seen in work on color-blind racism. Some have sought to understand the link between covert sentiment and behaviors that target migrants.[30] This effort has, in large part, validated the assertion implicit in this work: covert attitudes can affect covert acts. For example, an effort to understand the extension of citizenship in Switzerland revealed that attitudes correlated reasonably well with behavior.[31]

Herein lies the paradox. In a hypothetical world where xenophobes anticipate no social cost to overtly expressed intolerance, they would find little reason to avoid overtly xenophobic acts. Migrants can and do confront just such contexts—those in which masking is of no strategic value. In such a context, delineating overt and covert acts is of little meaning. However, if social norms shift and racism or ethnocentrism becomes subject to social and even legal repercussions, the multilayered model of the xenophobe offers a clear path for the perpetuation of intolerance. In fact, as the evidence in this chapter demonstrates for Ireland and the Netherlands, linking race or ethnicity to xenophobia *causes* the xenophobe to be limited to covert expressions of intolerance. Similarly, covert acts emerge as a refuge for the covert xenophobe only when overt acts are no longer available. This understanding reconfigures what would be a reasonable intervention or redress for observed patterns—albeit indirectly observed—of xenophobia rooted in race or ethnicity. As the cases of Ireland and the Netherlands underscore, the overt expression of tolerance is consistently expressed with little variation shown to be linked with the racial or ethnic identity of the migrant. Covert expression is a different story. In other words, the effect of the social stigmatization of racism or ethnocentrism is not accurately reflected in overtly expressed sentiment, nor would it be observed in associated acts.

CHANGING THE BEHAVIOR OF THE INTENTIONALLY MASKED XENOPHOBE

How do we interpret the effect of changes in attitudes and behavior if people don't always do what they say they will? This question is important for work that considers the role of race and ethnicity as a motive for xenophobia. Without offering a point-by-point assessment of policy meant to prevent racial and ethnic intolerance, there are some lessons to consider from the clear evidence of the substantial masking of intolerance—particularly when race or ethnicity is in the frame.

First, the evidence in this chapter indicates that policy focused on the reduction or elimination of speech or practices that negatively target people of a specific race or ethnicity should not be limited to overt acts. Overtly discriminatory migration policies such as Executive Order 13769, the U.S. ban on newcomers from a list of Muslim-majority countries,[32] are subject to legal and social regulation. This executive order was challenged but never overturned—instead, a replacement came into effect later that proved able to withstand legal challenge.[33] Hate speech is often similarly regulated (or attempted to be regulated) by U.S. states.[34] The emphasis in both cases is on overt acts and statements. As we know well now, such regulation can affect only the first layer of xenophobic expression. It is a limited intervention at best. Without needing to instantly shift to a focus on unconscious forms of prejudice, which is a notoriously problematic concept to define and measure,[35] the key takeaway from this chapter—and this book—is that patterns of overt speech systematically underestimate the existing prevalence of covert xenophobes, particularly when expressed intolerance intersects with race and ethnicity. The implication is that covert behavior is similarly preferred, strategically. In addition, racial and ethnic prejudice motivates a masking of antipathy toward migrants for those forced to acknowledge co-ethnicity with newcomers. As a result, interventions that seek to influence overt speech and acts are always going to be constrained because intentional and strategic masking is by definition a successful avoidance strategy.

Second, a clear and potentially effective strategy to mitigate the ability of intentionality to function as a covert mechanism to maintain xenophobia is the judicious use (or withholding) of anonymity. Extending the domains within which social stigma can be anticipated by racists and ethnocentrists reduces the number of moments or interactions in which their prejudicial preferences are relevant. Again, this type of approach is not akin to interventions to address unconscious biases, which the evidence suggests are of limited efficacy.[36] Instead, it is an acknowledgment that focusing exclusively on the overt xenophobe's links with racial and ethnic bigotry is limited and, as this chapter shows, counterproductive. Shining a light on the links between expressed intolerance toward immigrants and the race or ethnicity of the newcomer can increase the xenophobe's strategic preference for masking. In other words, targeting racism as a motive for xenophobia can result in it seeming as if racism is less of a concern because the covert xenophobe remains prevalent and active. In terms of acts, simple approaches to increase the access to information about interactions (e.g., performing external reviews, recording decision-making processes in hiring, blinding details of job applicants' race or ethnicity) are viable. All efforts to increase transparency do not equate to uniformly better practices in all cases, but efforts to consider the importance of social stigma and, moreover, reduce the number of contexts in which it can be avoided are well worth considering and empirically valid.

If there is one lesson to be learned here, it is that the somewhat reduced public space for race- and ethnicity-based xenophobia does not guarantee a reduction of intolerance in any absolute sense. Greater diversity in the migrant population can simultaneously embolden xenophobic expression and concentrate it in the realm of the intentionally masked. In-group and out-group identities can dramatically change the overt and covert contexts of reception. Linking migrant identity with race can lead to greater masking as a strategy to avoid the stigma of racialized or ethnocentric intolerance. The use of masking is moderated by the ethnic self-identification of members of receiving societies— as with Hispanic people in the United States. In other words, covert intolerance is less prevalent in contexts in which people of co-ethnic identity are present. By the same token, racial and ethnic out-group members in contexts with no co-ethnic communities are particularly vulnerable.

6

BEHIND A VEIL OF INTOLERANCE

Islamophobia and Overt Xenophobic Expression

T he Islamophobe embodies a targeted and potentially increasingly salient type of xenophobe. Islamophobic sentiment figures prominently in contentious debates over migration, religion, and society in many contexts of reception—both in Europe and elsewhere. We've already explored the ways that an economic crisis, political rhetoric, and race and ethnicity shape (and reshape) the strategy of expression deployed by the xenophobe in the United States, the United Kingdom, Ireland, and the Netherlands. If anything, the multilayered model of the xenophobe clarifies that social stigma operates differently depending on the context within which the sentiment is expressed. A consistent theme is concealment. The survey experiments described in the previous chapters point to important differences in the *extent* to which strategic masking is used by the xenophobe, particularly when social stigma is framed by attributes of the newcomer and the respondent. Most insightful is the observation that masking is often present in the absence of any clear mechanism to reduce the anticipated stigmatization of intolerance. To foreshadow what we'll uncover in this chapter, the Islamophobe is somewhat of an exception to this rule. With the Islamophobe, we'll confront how limited the pressure of anticipated stigmatization can be when the targeted newcomer is Muslim.

We'll consider multiple contexts, exploring results from list experiments conducted in the United States, the United Kingdom, Ireland, and the Netherlands. This comparative view reveals that the pressure to mask intolerance toward Muslim immigrants can be very low—nonexistent in some cases—when compared to that directed at other migrant groups. This evidence points toward an alarming trend. Despite limited differences in anonymously expressed opposition toward Muslim and non-Muslim migrants, Muslim migrants find themselves a disproportionately targeted category of newcomer for overtly xenophobic rhetoric. The evidence highlights an undeniable intersection of religion and xenophobia, which results in a near absence of any effort to conceal intolerance. In other words, the Islamophobe is mainstream—and openly so.

ISLAM AND MIGRATION

Migration from Muslim-majority countries to the United States and Europe has increased in recent years relative to the late twenty-first century.[1] Estimates suggest that Islam will become the fastest-growing religious group globally with the largest increases in terms of population found in the Asia-Pacific region.[2] In Europe, the Muslim population is projected to reach 10 percent of the total population in the next three decades,[3] although that figure is somewhat uncertain given the estimate's sensitivity to policy and demographic assumptions. In the United States, the total number of Muslims is expected to reach nearly 2.1 percent of the total population in the same period.[4] To put these data in context, the U.S. growth rate is notably slower than that observed in Europe and constitutes a smaller share of the total population than do atheists and agnostics, who made up 3.1 percent and 4.0 percent of the total population, respectively, in 2014. In short, Muslims—as a community and as a defined category of newcomer—should not be of particular note to the xenophobe because of their group size relative to the overall national or regional population.

Rather than reflecting a numbers game in which the largest population commands the greatest attention, Islam has become a prominent target of the contemporary xenophobe for reasons that blend present-day political trends and evolving perceptions of cultural competition.[5] As the rhetoric around the referendum in the United Kingdom to leave the European Union revealed (the racial and ethnic dimension of which was explored in chapter 4), borders and the type of migrant crossing them have proved to be effective political motives. As we'll see in this chapter, Islam, particularly when targeted after the 2015 refugee "crisis," played at least as important a role in Brexit politics as part of broader appeals to border control. The United States is similar to the United Kingdom in that, despite Muslim migrants being a small minority of the newcomer population relative to those from the Americas, a key policy initiative (i.e., Executive Order 13769) pushed for a near-total ban on arrivals from a list of Muslim-majority countries.[6] Islam as a religion and Muslim as an identity and practice were clearly targets for overt opposition for reasons that the size of the migration flow could not explain. In both contexts, overt opposition to Muslim newcomers was a key feature of contemporary tensions about migration more broadly, which speaks to the disproportionate influence religion played in shaping the debate.

This brief overview emphasizes two key details that have clear theoretical implications for our understanding of the anticipated stigma of xenophobic expression aimed at Muslims. First, a large Muslim community of reception is rarely present—at least at the national and regional level. Muslims constitute single-digit percentages of the populations of destination for most new arrivals from Muslim-majority countries in Europe and North America.[7] Second, Muslim migration is prominently discussed and opposed in many of these destination contexts—whether by way of political rhetoric or overtly targeted policy. Chapter 4 gave a much more detailed overview of the link between this openly expressed xenophobia and populist political successes, but it is necessary here to highlight the fact that Islamophobic rhetoric is a frequently observed flavor of xenophobia in contemporary contexts. This type of xenophobia is distinct from expressed intolerance rooted in racism or ethnocentrism, which we've seen is frequently present only when anonymity is available.

THE CONFLUENCE OF
ISLAMOPHOBIA AND XENOPHOBIA

Before moving to case studies, it is worth describing, albeit briefly, the links between the xenophobe and the Islamophobe. As with racism, considering Islamophobia as a category of xenophobia and the Islamophobe as a type of xenophobe does not suggest that the former is less impactful. Quite the contrary. As we consider the links between general xenophobia and more targeted Islamophobia, it is well worth keeping in mind that the theoretically broad umbrella that the xenophobe encapsulates does not relegate other dimensions—like Islamophobia—to a role of lesser importance. This point was made in the discussion of racially and ethnically motivated xenophobes. The multilayered model of the xenophobe articulated in this book has consistently underlined the fact that the target and strategy of expression pursued by the xenophobe are inextricably shaped by the context within which the sentiment is expressed. In other words, knowing to *whom* the xenophobe intends to express antipathy is key and, in many instances, the single most salient marker of context, thereby providing notable insight into the distinct layers of xenophobic expression (i.e., overt versus covert).

The Islamophobe shares all the broad dimensions of the xenophobe as captured by the three layers of the multilayered model of xenophobic expression but is distinguished by the singular target of antipathy: the Muslim. To understand what this means for the articulation of Islamophobia, it is easiest to draw from cases in which the logic of intolerance was similarly narrowed to a specific frame. Consider materialist (chapter 3) or race-based (chapter 5) forms of intolerance. In both cases, the logic of opposition—economic competition or threat in the case of the former and racism in the case of the latter—built from a standpoint that emphasized a particular attribute of the newcomer. These specific characteristics became the pathway by which intolerance found expression. In the case of materialist concerns, an economic crisis led to more overt expression, but expression at the second layer, which is intentionally and consciously masked, remained unchanged. Similarly, racialized antipathy was reluctantly expressed and notably more similar across groups for overt expression. Only when anonymity was offered did variation emerge.

With that premise, let's consider Islam as a motive for intolerance in migrant receiving contexts. The examples in academic scholarship are many, but few account for the masking of intolerance, so the view is limited. In the United States,[8] in Europe,[9] and from the perspective of international comparative work,[10] one broad conclusion stands out: Muslims are a clear and disproportionate target of intolerance. At the risk of oversimplification, the general finding is that Muslims, specifically Muslim migrants, in most contexts of reception are confronted with targeted antipathy. Islamophobia is widely observed and widely practiced. Similarly, the Islamophobe confronts many circumstances unique to a place and time, as demonstrated by the various historical patterns that have brought Muslim migrants to a variety of contexts of reception, ranging from guest worker programs to historical colonial ties and from family reunification to refugee flows.

Although there is somewhat of a consensus—or as much of one as is ever found in social science—that the Islamophobe is a stable feature of contemporary receiving societies, the link between the Islamophobe and the xenophobe is contested. For example, consider the case of dress, specifically the perception of how Muslim women "should" dress. Some work finds that religiosity is of particular salience but only as a determinant of general opposition rather than any clear antipathy toward Muslim dress (e.g., a headscarf).[11] In contrast, in other contexts, it is found that dress is the trigger for antipathy but not in a clearly targeted way, suggesting that general antipathy toward migration (i.e., generalized xenophobia) overlaps significantly with antipathy directed at Muslims and that the two should be considered in tandem to some extent.[12] The key takeaway from this body of research can best be summarized as a blurring of the distinction in the mind of the Islamophobe between specific triggers and broader forms of intolerance such as nonspecific antireligious sentiment or generalized antimigrant sentiment). To be even more succinct, the Islamophobe might be just a selective expression of xenophobia rather than a separate construct. This framing could place it in a subservient role to or as a coequal of the xenophobe. We'll explore this idea in some detail here.

Nearly all work takes Islamophobes at "face value." But as previous chapters have repeatedly shown, we do this at our own peril. The obvious shortcoming of this approach is that if the Islamophobe confronts less stigma than incurred with other types of antipathy (e.g., racism), what appears to be targeted antipathy, seen as distinct from other forms of xenophobic expression, is really limited to that which is overtly expressed. This point is a consistent caveat in this book, but the case of the Islamophobe is truly a cautionary tale. Does the Islamophobe take the path of least resistance, or does the Islamophobe sincerely harbor greater intolerance toward Muslims relative to, for example, groups with shared attributes (e.g., coreligionists, groups of co-ethnic identity). To explore this possibility, let's now turn to four contexts of reception: the United States, the United Kingdom, the Netherlands, and Ireland.

ISLAM AND CITIZENSHIP IN THE UNITED STATES

The rise of Islamophobia in the United States provides insight into a context in which Muslims are a small minority, albeit a slowly growing one. Yet Islamophobic attitudes have often been part of the mainstream political and social discourse in recent decades. As chapter 5 revealed, in the United States migration and Hispanic identity are intimately intertwined. Latin America—and the U.S. equivalent in terms of identity (i.e., Hispanic)—have come to define the migrant, which was reflected in the distinct layering of xenophobia found in research among self-identifying Hispanics in the United States. But the meaning of this finding for other types of newcomers—and there are many—depends on the degree to which additional factors make certain group characteristics more visible. In the case of Muslims, the conversation has been driven by more than two decades of marquee, often violent, events that created an outsized impression decoupled from population size or patterns of migration. The perception of Islam and Muslims among the U.S. general public is rarely, if ever, informed by any sustained direct interaction.

In the United States, Muslims constitute less than 1 percent of the country's population but often garner significant attention in the media and political discourse because Muslim-majority countries have played (or have been perceived to have played) a role in instances of violence ranging from the hostage crisis during the Iranian Revolution of 1978–1979, to the terrorist attacks of September 11, 2001, to resistance to occupation in Iraq starting in 2003.[13] These concrete cases of conflict have been coupled with a near-uniform negative stereotyping of Muslims in popular culture.[14] The result is that about 60 percent of Muslims in the United States have reported discrimination, misunderstanding, and stereotyping to be some of the most important concerns they confront.[15] As shown in chapters 3 and 5, when considering the broader question of the U.S. border and race-based preferences, survey respondents are aware of aware of the stigma associated with expressing intolerant attitudes toward different groups of migrants. This finding is evidenced by the intentional masking observed when anonymity changes the extent to which intolerance is overtly or covertly expressed. The key insight here is that attitudes are already formed. Similarly—but perhaps more so— Muslims confront a context in which the general population, independent of any direct contact in many cases, is more than able to articulate their views. The extent to which these preexisting attitudes are overtly or covertly expressed is another matter.

Again, we turn to anonymity to reveal the layers of the U.S. Islamophobe. As in all experiments conducted for this book, participants in a randomized and representative survey experiment were queried about their attitudes using direct questioning and via the list experiment, which provided permanent and absolute anonymity (see chapter 2 for a detailed overview of the technique). In this case, two types of targeted antipathy were framed. The first frame pertained to legal (i.e., documented) Muslim migrants. The second frame was identical except for the target group being legal Christian migrants. A list experiment was used for each to measure covertly expressed sentiment. The results permitted overt sentiment, targeting both Muslim and Christian migrants, to be distinguished from and directly compared with covert sentiment. The frames targeted naturalization, defined as migrants having been granting citizenship, which intentionally highlighted a bright line for legal in-group membership. In addition, defining both groups as legal residents avoided conflation with sentiment directed at the undocumented population, which is a contested definition of newcomer in the United States. The result was an ability to isolate, to an extent, the independent role of religion in shaping xenophobic and Islamophobic sentiment. This list experiment entered the field in parallel with one focused on a closed border (described in chapter 3; see that chapter for a description of the sample and mode of data collection). Detailed results from this experiment were published with my collaborator Amaney Jamal in 2015 (see appendix 4 for a detailed overview of the experimental design).[16]

Table 6.1 offers a succinct summary of the results. The second column reveals a large gap in the estimated percentage of the population who overtly opposed citizenship for legal Muslim and legal Christian migrants. Thirty percent of the sample openly opposed citizenship for legal Muslim migrants, but only 11 percent openly opposed citizenship for legal Christian migrants. The implication of this finding is that a fairly large percentage of the U.S. general population are overtly Islamophobic in terms

TABLE 6.1 OVERT AND COVERT OPPOSITION TO CITIZENSHIP FRAMED BY RELIGION IN THE UNITED STATES

	Overt	Participants	Covert	Participants	Percentage who mask Overt–covert
Muslim	30%*	623	33%*	620	–3%
Christian	11%*	623	28%*	585	–17%*

Source: TESS-Experiments, "Perceptions of Islam, Migration, and Citizenship in the United States: A List Experiment," Open Science Framework, October 20, 2021, osf.io/74ahy

Note: The overt questions were worded as follows: "Do you support or oppose granting citizenship to a legal immigrant who is Muslim?" and "Do you support or oppose granting citizenship to a legal immigrant who is Christian?" The covert question was worded similarly but administered such that no direct indication of support or opposition was required. (See chapter 2 for a more detailed description of the technique and appendix 4 for the full text of all questions.) In the table, * indicates that the reported percentage is significantly different from zero (p ≤ 0.10).

of religion determining opposition without any need for additional details in the frame. Put another way, if you are a Muslim migrant, you can expect to confront about three times the opposition to your naturalization than if you are a Christian migrant.

Of course, we do not stop here. The insight and power of the multilayered model of xenophobic expression is that overt sentiment is only one face of the xenophobe. The "Covert" column of table 6.1 shows another. This column provides the percentage of the sample opposed to citizenship when permanent and absolute anonymity was provided. Reflecting the second layer of xenophobic expression, these estimates prove to be remarkably insightful in the case of the Islamophobe. Compared to the percentage who expressed overt opposition to legal Muslim migrants, the percentage who expressed covert was nearly unchanged. This is one of the few cases we'll encounter in this book when anonymity does not reveal a distinct pattern. The implication of this finding is that the anticipation of social stigma is of little consequence so long as the target of antipathy is Muslim. Another way to think about this is that Islamophobia is seen as socially acceptable in the United States.

In sharp contrast, antipathy toward Christian migrants differed dramatically when anonymity relieved the pressure of social stigma. Whereas only 11 percent of respondents expressed overt opposition to the Christian frame, this frame elicited nearly three times the opposition when anonymity was provided. This increase, when compared to sentiment directed toward legal Muslim migrants, is insightful for two reasons. First, the expression of opposition to citizenship for Christian migrants is clearly stigmatized. In fact, the difference between overt and covert sentiment directed toward Christian migrants was nearly identical to the difference between overt opposition for Muslim and Christian migrants. This point brings us to a second insight: covert antipathy directed toward Christian and Muslim migrants was notably similar at 28 percent and 33 percent, respectively.

The seemingly straightforward narrative of the Islamophobe is evidently an interpretation that is limited to openly expressed opposition. The Islamophobe is a feature of the first layer of the multilayered model but not the second. Instead, the second layer, characterized by consciously masked intolerance, indicates that the prevalence of Islamophobes in the U.S. population is indistinguishable from that of anti-Christian xenophobes. A blanket generalization that Muslims are a unique target of intolerance in all domains does not hold. Instead, the Islamophobe is better understood as a reflection of the limited consequences for those who overtly express targeted intolerance in the United States. The U.S. Islamophobe is, in essence, a manifestation of how intolerance is presented rather than an immutable core feature of xenophobia—independent of context or strategy.

Context matters. The Islamophobe is clearly sensitive to context and adapts—or rather elects no strategic change—as a direct result. What we might (mis)interpret as Islamophobia, full stop, is better understood as a reaction to a specific context and resulting strategy. If that is the case and if context defines the extent to which Islamophobia defines the overt xenophobe, what happens when the context changes? To understand this, we return to Brexit.

ISLAM, BORDERS, AND BREXIT

Chapter 4 focused on the political mainstreaming of intolerance. Without retreading well-covered terrain, let's focus on the aspect of the Brexit debate that targeted Muslim migrants. One example was the foregrounding of Turkey in the campaign to support the United Kingdom's exit from the European Union. A standard image used in the official Vote Leave campaign was simply an a red background with an estimate of Turkey's current population overlayed with the phrase "Turkey is joining the EU."[17] Given that interest in Turkey joining the European Union was limited at that time, reflected in mostly stalled chapters for admission and limited support in both Turkish and EU public opinion, the message would have come as a surprise to all those involved. There was certainly no plausible scenario in which Turkey would join the European Union in the near or medium term—if ever. The imagery reflected a key dimension of the Brexit debate, in which depicting migration as a contributor to material precarity was of limited interest. Instead, it was claimed that the real threat, as often overtly articulated by those hoping the United Kingdom would exit the European Union, was religion, and the religion was Islam. This focus does not mean that other types of xenophobic discourse were absent from the debate, but migration moved to the fore—whether it be Muslim-majority refugee migration or simply unrestricted movement from a Muslim-majority country upon entrance into the European Union. The emphasis on migration was seen online in a notable uptick in the volume and prevalence of Islamophobic discourse.[18] Some have gone as far as to suggest that negative portrayals of Muslim men linked to refugee migration constituted the primary emotional appeal of the pro-Brexit campaign.[19]

This mainstreaming of intolerance, specifically targeted at Muslim newcomers to the United Kingdom, confronted an equally spirited, although ultimately unsuccessful, campaign to keep the United Kingdom in the European Union. As shown in chapter 4, linkages were made between opposition to the European Union and sociocultural intolerance (e.g., racism, Islamophobia).[20] The result was a competition of messages and a polarized public square in which most overt attitudes that touched on the topic of Brexit could anticipate some degree of stigmatization by supporters of one side of the issue or the other.

As mentioned, when it was first introduced, the list experiment used in the study of Brexit was designed in collaboration with Amaney Jamal, and detailed results were published in 2022 (see appendix 2 for a detailed overview of the experimental design).[21]

Table 6.2 shows only the results from the list experiment that capture overt and covert attitudes toward Muslim migration. The insight here is of a rapidly shifting sociopolitical context and the resulting change in strategy deployed by the Islamophobe. Nearly identical to what was found in the United States, the pre-Brexit sentiment directed at Muslim migrants, shown in the first row, was notably unaffected by the provision of anonymity. The interpretation of this finding is that, as with the U.S. results shown in table 6.1, there is little evidence that social stigma translated into

TABLE 6.2 SUPPORT FOR MUSLIM MIGRANTS TO THE UNITED KINGDOM BEFORE AND AFTER BREXIT

			Percentage who mask
	Overt	Covert	Overt–covert
Pre-Brexit	46%*	43%*	3%
Post-Brexit	52%*	37%*	15%*

Source: University of Essex, Institute for Social and Economic Research. *Understanding Society: Innovation Panel*, Wave 8 and Wave 9, 2015–2016 [data collection] 11th Edition, 2021. UK Data Service. SN: 6849, http://doi.org/10.5255/UKDA-SN-6849-14.

Note: The overt question was worded as follows: "Do you think the UK should allow people from Muslim countries to come and live here?" The covert question was worded similarly but administered such that no direct indication of support or opposition was required. (See chapter 2 for a more detailed description of the technique and appendix 2 for the full text of all questions.) In the table, * indicates that the reported percentage was significantly different from zero ($p \leq 0.10$). (For the key dates of the Brexit timeline, see table 4.1.)

a strategic concealment of targeted opposition or an overstatement of support for Muslim migrants. If you recall from chapter 4, about 20 percent of UK survey respondents overstated their support for Caribbean and Eastern European migrants, suggesting that the absence of social stigma was unique to Muslim migrants—just as in the case of citizenship in the United States. If we ignore the post-Brexit results, this pattern reinforces the conclusion that the Islamophobe is best understood as a unique manifestation of the strategic xenophobe.

However, Brexit changed the landscape, proving once again that context does indeed matter and is far from stable. The contested and highly emotive campaigns resulted in a situation in which overt and targeted antipathy toward Muslims became a form of expression that, subsequent to the vote, could anticipate stigma. The absence of a difference between overt and covert sentiment significantly and substantively widened to reach a gap of 15 percentage points, as shown in table 6.2, which is the difference between overt and covert sentiment in the survey experiment. Moreover, overt support for Muslim migrants actually went *up*. Overtly, the UK general population expressed *greater* tolerance after Brexit, which was broadly interpreted as a key victory for a political constituency defined by a stridently more restrictionist border policy. This uptick paralleled a clear-cut decline in covert support. What should be obvious by now is how little there is to be learned by observing only overt sentiment. That first layer of intolerance is impactful and worth acknowledging but offers only a limited view of the behavior of the xenophobe in practice. In this case, if assessing only the first layer, one might be left with the impression that Brexit softened the UK population's attitudes toward Muslim migrants. Instead, the narrative is a bit more complex, and covert support for Muslim migrants declined notably. What Brexit did, among other things, was stigmatize the Islamophobe. The same pressures that made Islamophobia strategically preferable and a candidate for overt expression worked against it in the post-Brexit period.

EDUCATION AND THE MASKED ISLAMOPHOBE IN THE NETHERLANDS AND IRELAND

The case of Brexit highlights how the Islamophobe is, in many ways, a manifestation of context and strategy. The pressures of stigma can shape the way that intolerance is strategically masked and, within a short period of time (e.g., Brexit), create overtly more tolerant and covertly less tolerant attitudes—in parallel. This guiding hand can be seen as a period effect, like that shown earlier for an economic crisis and the resulting appeal of materialist narratives of intolerance. However, the Islamophobe is also shaped by factors that contribute to our understanding of the stigma associated with targeted intolerance. This notion is different from interpreting a change in context (e.g., Brexit). Rather, Islamophobia is a process of socialization that can occur much earlier in the life course, most commonly through education. Much as the literature has shown education to be an institutional context that shapes our understanding of the rules of social and economic mobility,[22] the experience of education provides a hidden curriculum of the norms governing intolerance.

Approaches to understanding the determinants of opposition to migration and migrants never drift far from a consideration of education. That said, the meaning of education is contested. Some suggest it is a marker of labor-market position or human capital investment and as such a proxy for a perception of economic threat attributable to new entrants into a labor market.[23] This materialist perspective stands in contrast to a perspective that emphasizes the relative tolerance derived from greater educational attainment—whether via a process of selection or conditioning or exposure.[24] Some have pointed out that accounting for cultural values and beliefs can fully explain the association between education and antipathy toward migrants.[25] Others suggest that education is better understood as a marker of cultural capital rather than a materialist notion of human capital.[26] Of course, materialist and sociocultural interpretations need not be mutually exclusive.[27]

One near-universal pattern is that more education translates into more tolerance. Whether this implies a better labor-market position or a more cosmopolitan outlook need not be clear to see the gradient emerge. In terms of Islamophobia, some work in the Netherlands has found that less education predicts a greater perception that Islam is a threat.[28] In general, regardless of the interpretation of educational attainment, the less educated are expected to express less tolerance, and vice versa. What this perspective fails to anticipate, however, is that education also shapes our ability to anticipate stigma. The more educated are potentially exposed to (or selected for) notions of tolerance because educational environments—particularly secondary and tertiary (i.e., college or university)—provide an introduction to the hidden rules of society. Students learn to navigate the often unspoken expectations that chart pathways of social and economic mobility. But does this exposure to a hidden curriculum lead to a greater sensitivity to the stigmatization of intolerance? Are the more educated more tolerant in all domains or simply more strategic in their expression of intolerance?

To answer these questions, let's consider two contexts—the Netherlands and Ireland—that offer distinct views of the interplay between the xenophobe and the Islamophobe. The Netherlands has an extensive history with migration from Muslim-majority countries.[29] Ireland, in contrast, has a long history as a migrant-sending context, and net immigration is a relatively new phenomenon for the country. The Netherlands, in terms of overt expression, presents contradictory views on Muslim newcomers. Only 35 percent of the population of the Netherlands has a negative view of Muslims, which is notably less than in other European contexts (e.g., Greece, Hungary, Italy, Poland),[30] but the majority consider Islam and Dutch culture to be incompatible.[31] This latter tendency is highlighted by the support enjoyed by the Party for Freedom, an overtly anti-Muslim political party. This contradiction was alluded to in chapter 5, but more to the point here is the fact that overtly expressed attitudes in the Netherlands indicate a clear gradient with those with more than secondary-level education being twice as likely as those who did not complete secondary school to express a more tolerant position.[32] In Ireland, on the other hand, the issue of Muslim newcomers is relatively recent and of far less salience. The Muslim community in Ireland constitutes less than 2 percent of the Irish population,[33] is highly educated,[34] and is notably diverse in terms of country or context of origin and racial or ethnic self-identification.[35]

To assess the role of education in shaping overt and covert expressions of Islamophobic sentiment, let's consider two broadly comparable survey experiments conducted in the Netherlands and Ireland (table 6.3). Both used similarly worded frames to consider attitudes toward Muslim migrants. Also, both employed a list experiment to provide absolute and permanent anonymity, thereby offering insight into attitudes free from anticipated stigma. (Chapter 2 provides an overview of this approach.) Some results from Irish survey experiment were published in collaboration with Frances McGinnity and Éamonn Fahey in partnership with the Irish Human Rights and Equality Commission in 2020 and 2022.[36] Some results from the list experiment in the Netherlands were published in 2019 (in collaboration with Philip Brenner, Peter Schmidt, and Diana Zavala-Rojas) and 2020 (see appendix 4 for a detailed overview of the experimental designs used in Ireland and the Netherlands).[37] The key addition in this chapter is a disaggregation by level of education. The survey in the Netherlands considered a graduated set of educational categories, whereas the survey in Ireland delineated individuals who had attained a college or university education from those who had not.

We'll ignore the covert results for the moment, limiting our focus to the second column, which reports overt support for Muslim migrants. The pattern suggests that Islamophobes are overrepresented among the less educated. This finding fits the standard narrative in the literature that attributes greater intolerance to the less educated—whether it targets Muslims or migrants more broadly. In addition, tertiary education (and

TABLE 6.3 SUPPORT FOR MUSLIM MIGRANTS TO THE NETHERLANDS AND IRELAND BY LEVEL OF EDUCATION

	Overt	Covert	Percentage who mask (Overt–covert)
The Netherlands			
Overall	44%*	27%*	18%*
Primary	40%*	28%*	12%
Lower secondary	26%*	21%*	6%
Upper secondary	55%*	27%*	28%*
Junior college	37%*	21%*	16%*
College or university	60%*	34%*	26%*
Ireland			
Overall	56%*	48%*	8%
Less than college or university	50%*	49%*	1%
College, university, or postgraduate	63%*	48%*	15%*

Source: M. Creighton, L. Lilleoja, P. Schmidt, and D. Zavala-Rojas, CentERdata, LISS panel—List experiment on social desirability bias in attitudes towards immigration. DANS 2019. https://doi.org/10.17026/dans-zw3-btmr; M. J. Creighton, É. Fahey, and F. McGinnity, "Immigration, Identity, and Anonymity: Intentionally Masked Intolerance in Ireland," *International Migration Review* 56, no. 3 (2022): 881–910. https://doi.org/10.1177/01979183211054806.

Note: In the Netherlands, the overt question was worded as follows: "Do you think the Netherlands should allow people from Muslim countries to come and live here?" In Ireland, the overt question was worded as follows: "Do you support more Muslim people coming to live in Ireland?" For both countries, the covert questions were worded similarly but administered such that no direct indication of support or opposition was required. The educational categories are not directly comparable; therefore, the results are reported separately for each country. (See chapter 2 for a more detailed description of the technique and appendix 4 for the full text of all questions.) In the table, * indicates that the reported percentage was significantly different from zero (p ≤ 0.10).

upper-secondary education to a lesser extent) was found to be a dividing line, with 60 percent of those with a college or university education indicating support for Muslim migrants but only 26 percent of those with a lower-secondary education indicating support. Similarly, the results for Ireland show a somewhat steep increase in tolerance among the most educated, with 63 percent of those with a college, university, or postgraduate education reporting overt support for Muslim migrants. But support dropped to 50 percent among those with less than a college or university education. Also of note, the percentage expressing support among the most educated was somewhat similar in Ireland and the Netherlands—at least in terms of overt sentiment—although more contexts would need be considered before much could be concluded from this similarity.

Now let's turn our attention to the role of education in the presence of absolute anonymity, as shown in the column of table 6.3 labeled "Covert." Here, the pattern is notably different. Rather than a clear gradient with tolerance increasing along with attained education, differences between levels of education in both contexts were less or, in the case of Ireland, absent altogether. Moreover, the pattern of strategic masking was concentrated among the more educated, which is shown by the difference between overt and covert sentiment in the last column of table 6.3. In fact, the less educated in the Netherlands and Ireland did not show any meaningful concealment of intolerance toward Muslim migrants. There is some evidence of an erosion of support between overt and covert sentiment, at least among those with a primary education, but it is nothing like that seen for those with an upper-secondary or tertiary education in the Netherlands, which decline from 55 percent and 60 percent to 27 percent and 34 percent, respectively. This finding largely eliminates the differences between primary, lower-secondary, upper-secondary, and tertiary schooling in the Netherlands. Ireland is similar in that those with a tertiary education expressed near-identical covert support for Muslim migrants to that expressed by those with less education: 48 percent and 49 percent, respectively.

The lessons here are twofold. First, as in the cases of the financial crisis in the United States and the pre-Brexit period in the United Kingdom, Islamophobia is an overt phenomenon. The Islamophobe, relative to those who fear strangers framed in other ways, is very much out in the open. In addition, when expressed overtly, Islamophobia is concentrated among the less educated. Second, the overt pattern is not paralleled by covert expression. What seems to be a targeted preference is more of a gradient in strategic masking, with the better educated masking to a greater extent. In terms of covert expression, the less and more educated are far more similar. In the case of Ireland, the difference between overt and covert expression was somewhat indistinguishable. Relative tolerance among the more educated appears to be surface level—limited to the first and outermost layer of the multilayered xenophobe. Once other layers are accounted for, the more educated are no longer disproportionately tolerant but instead are uniquely strategic. The message here is that education results in a greater understanding and anticipation of the social stigma of overtly expressed intolerance. A plausible explanation for this finding is that the hidden curriculum that formal education provides leads to greater facility with strategic impression management. This conclusion is different from one that finds that the less educated are inherently less tolerant in all contexts of interaction. Overt sentiment is impactful and meaningful, but it is not the whole story.

AN EXCEPTION TO THE BAND OF "OTHERS"

We now can see the Islamophobe as a more coherent social actor who does not match widely accepted narratives of the relationship between context and tolerance. The previous five chapters have consistently shown that many or most contexts of reception are normatively defined by at least some pressure to avoid overtly targeted intolerance. It is only when certain narratives (e.g., the perceived objectivity of economic necessity) become available that the xenophobe shifts toward more overt forms of expression. Islamophobia, however, is different. Being overtly opposed to Muslim migrants, even if Muslim identity is the only salient attribute in the frame, is viewed as a low-stigma or, in some cases, stigma-free form of xenophobia—at least in some important contexts of reception. Exceptional circumstances like Brexit or socialization via formal education can result in some masking of antipathy toward Muslim newcomers, but the general takeaway here is that the Islamophobe is a manifestation of intolerance that is rarely masked.

To understand the meaning of the limited stigmatization of Islamophobia, think of stigma as a form of social protection. At least in interactions in which overt forms of expression are the only option, social stigma can create a facade of acceptance and limits the perception of intergroup conflict—forming a sort of protective barrier from the brunt of overt intolerance. As mentioned in previous chapters, limited masking does not mean that the behavioral outcomes of targeted intolerance (e.g., discriminatory hiring, anti-immigrant voting) are absent or even plausibly less prevalent. But the stigmatization of overtly expressed Islamophobia does offer a more limited exposure to intolerance in day-to-day interactions. This respite, albeit limited, is demonstrably unavailable in some contexts to Muslim newcomers.

The significantly open expression of the Islamophobe indicates that masking is of no strategic benefit in many overt interactions. This lack of masking could be a consequence of the relatively small community affected by the Islamophobe, with even the most optimistic projections of population growth placing the Muslim population in Europe at 10 percent or less and in the United States well below 5 percent well into the future. Ireland is lower still at less than 2 percent.[38] It is perhaps because of this relatively small community that social norms, which are negotiated within meaningful social contexts and governed by plausible systems of social sanctioning, anticipate little that would be seen as problematic in overtly directing antipathy toward Muslims. Other groups, even if some attributes might clearly delineate an out-group, can find strength in numbers when day-to-day interactions might not happen outside moments of plausible observation by in-group members. When spaces are made more inclusive, it remains hard to assess what might be said without the anticipation of stigma.

Another consequence of the limited stigmatization of Islamophobia is that potential allies fail to find one other. Instead, the narrative indicates that Muslims are perceived as different. This narrative is true in many instances in which overt intolerance is disproportionately directed at Muslim migrants. However, the case of the United States shows that Muslim and Christian migrants are the recipients of differing levels of support only when support is overtly expressed (see table 6.1). Covertly expressed support is nearly identical, which indicates that both groups are perceived somewhat similarly at the level of the xenophobe when anonymity provides shelter from the stigma of intolerance. The implication of this finding is that in terms of covert xenophobia, Muslims might have a common experience with other groups that might appear protected when only overt sentiment is considered.

7

PEOPLE, IMMIGRANTS,
AND REFUGEES

CATEGORIES OF NEED

Although the line can be blurred, refugees are frequently distinguished from other types of newcomers by the absence of plausible agency. Any definition of a refugee overlaps with notions of forced migration and the narratives of displacement. As such, refugees can and should elicit sympathy in that there is a moral impetus to offer support as one would hope for the same if one were similarly situated. At the same time, the conveyance of a right to cross international borders often invites a significant level of scrutiny and protracted verification processes. In other words, the moral frame does not necessarily trump the caution and state-centric oversight that border crossing and, moreover, rights of residence can entail. The national view is not the only one of interest, although in practice it can be dominant because international systems of governance, primary among them the United Nations Refugee Agency, provide definitional parameters and convey legitimacy to certain categories of need. The most frequently referenced definition of *refugee* comes from the 1951 Refugee Convention: "someone who is unable or unwilling to return to their country of origin owing to a well-founded fear of being persecuted for reasons of race, religion, nationality, membership of a particular social group, or political opinion." A notable omission is material deprivation, which highlights the limits placed on who qualifies or does not qualify as a person in sufficient need to be considered a legal refugee. For example, one can never be poor enough to be a refugee. Similarly, although upheaval in the form of armed conflict can result in refugee status being conferred, climate change or environmental degradation would not similarly qualify.

In 2020, an estimated 26.4 million refugees were under some form of United Nations mandate,[1] and an additional 4.1 million were seeking asylum,[2] some of whom will eventually qualify as refugees. In Europe, there have been two significant sources of refugees in the past decade: Syria and, more recently, Ukraine. It is worth reflecting on the violence underpinning each context. Syrian refugees fled (and continue to flee) violence that escalated following a brutal crackdown on widespread antigovernment demonstrations in 2011. In the decade that followed, as the country descended into a protracted civil war fueled by arms and soldiers from the United States and Russia, the conflict resulted in 6.6 million refugees of whom 3.6 million currently reside in Turkey.[3] At the time of writing, the Syrian refugee diaspora is the largest international displacement on Earth and has held that top spot since 2014.

Ukraine emerged as a source of refugees in 2022. The invasion of the country by Russia on February 24 of that year has resulted in a protracted conflict and an exodus across the border. Most recent estimates put the number of people displaced to neighboring countries at 3.6 million, with a further 6.5 million displaced within Ukraine's borders. The situation continues to evolve rapidly, and the scale of the flow from Ukraine to other European states remains—and will remain—unpredictable.

It is entirely possible that the duration and magnitude of the displacement of Ukrainians because of the Russian invasion could equal or surpass those of Syria. One reason might be the notable difference in acceptance of asylum seekers from Ukraine relative to those from Syria—or any other country of origin for that matter.[4] Many European countries have few restrictions on residency, which indicates that many displaced Ukrainians who enter EU countries will quickly be considered refugees. That said, the conflict is unfolding, and comparisons with more established refugee flows are difficult. We'll return to the differences in reception between Ukrainian and Syrian refugees later, but both clearly deserve mention in any overview because both countries account for the largest and most salient flows of asylum seekers and refugees to Europe in recent memory.

In the case of Syria, there are some key differences that are useful to contrast with the more recent case of Ukraine. The land border between Syria and Europe is with Turkey, which finds itself once again in the position of being a bridge between southern Anatolia, Muslim-majority Mediterranean states, and southern Europe. For many fleeing the conflict in Syria, at least initially, Turkey was a means to an end, viewed as a country of transit—not the initial or final destination of choice. Notably distinct from the posture of much of Europe to the conflict in Ukraine was the reluctance and, in some cases, resistance within the European Union to supporting asylum claims originating in the conflict in Syria, which resulted in a 2016 "deal" between the European Union and Turkey. The result was a monetary and procedural arrangement such that Turkey became an unanticipated place of longer-term settlement[5] because financial incentives were provided to the Turkish government to limit the transit of migrants seeking to apply for asylum upon entering an EU member state. In addition, a process of dubious legality sought to return asylum seekers entering the European Union to Turkey—without review—in exchange for asylum seekers seeking to register within Turkey. This process had notably minimal impact but has resulted in striking examples of the European Union preventing potential refugees who are physically present in the European Union from even applying for asylum before being involuntarily removed.

Despite efforts to limit access to the European Union via land borders by way of a formal arrangement with Turkey, asylum claims originating in the conflict in Syria remain a fixture of the landscape in the European Union and Europe more broadly. Clearly, the effectiveness of an EU strategy rooted in a tenuous political arrangement, which included perceived guarantees (e.g., meaningful progression of Turkey's candidacy to be an EU state), was limited: the program was unevenly implemented and had little success. Migrants continue to file for asylum and continue to enter the European Union seeking to qualify as refugees. The reason is clear: the need to leave unsafe countries remains regardless of the European Union's political machinations. The result has been framed as a "crisis" by some, and tensions demonstrably rose within the European Union when member states expressed and acted upon diverging views of their obligations to support a centralized refugee resettlement scheme. This source of tension remains a fixture of internal EU politics because some countries accept the reallocation of asylum seekers from border countries (e.g., Greece), and others do not.[6]

The key issue here is the perception of need. How receiving contexts interpret the *deservedness* of asylum seekers and refugees is evidently linked to narratives of necessity that can, in a legal sense, be linked to an objective verification of an experience of conflict, deprivation, or systematic repression. These standards, codified in widely used international frameworks like the 1951

Refugee Convention, might leave the impression that there is an agreed-upon category of need and that contexts of reception act consistently when presented with a qualifying case. However, as shown in the substantial discrepancy between the rapid and minimal vetting of Ukrainian asylum seekers and the relatively arduous vetting and limited access provided by the European Union to those affected by the conflict in Syria, similarly deserving potential refugees experience very different welcomes when crossing a European border. Clearly, the patterning of policy and the lived experience of potential refugees, who originate in distinct contexts of origin, indicate that the view of refugees and the experience of being a refugee varies significantly within Europe. Legal or moral need can conflict with other considerations, particularly in the case of Syria, a Muslim-majority country. As chapter 6 underlined, Islam results in notably different patterns in the expression of overt and covert antipathy compared with other migrant attributes. The intersection among Islam, refugee migration, and perception of need can and does shape how support—or opposition—is expressed.

CONTRASTING CATEGORIES OF NEED: REFUGEES AND MUSLIM NEWCOMERS IN NORWAY

By definition, refugee migration is unpredictable and driven by some of the most tragic and volatile circumstances imaginable. At the time of writing, it is increasingly clear that Ukraine, which was not on the radar as a source of refugees until very recently, has come to drive the conversation and dominate the public perception of displaced people in Europe. For many years before, this position in the minds of the public in European contexts of reception was held by Syrians. As a result, Islam was intimately intertwined with the public's perception of who constituted an asylum seeker. As with the case of Latin America migrants to the United States (see chapter 5), the salient attributes of newcomers—of which religion figures prominently in the case of Syria and Europe—become the "face" of all migrants to a degree. This near-blanket association anchors distinct layers of in-group and out-group identification because the relevant characteristics of the contexts of origin become ingrained as dominant attributes of the new arrivals in the psyche of general public in receiving contexts. Independent of refugee status, we've already seen that Muslim migrants to the United States and the United Kingdom are perceived quite differently from Christian migrants (see chapter 6) and Eastern European migrants (see chapter 4). What is less appreciated is whether these distinctions are mitigated by refugee status. Does qualification for a legal and moral category of need mitigate the often-observed targeted opposition to Muslim newcomers in European contexts? Does the presence of refugee status increase the social stigma of opposition? These questions focus on the strategic approach taken by the xenophobe when a clear category of need is understood to be applicable.

The case of Norway provides unique insight because this country is a context in which the economic turmoil of the 2007–2008 financial crisis was substantially buffered by a robust welfare state.[7] Norway's policies of social support might have mitigated the worst of the economic downturn, but the politics of migration in Norway were (and remain) somewhat contentious. A case in point is when one of the largest political parties, the Progress Party, which formed part of the governing coalition at the time, withdrew its support for the government in 2020 over the issue of refugees from the Syrian conflict. The opposition to arrivals from the Syrian conflict was not plausibly limited to a definitional quarrel over who should constitute a refugee because the Progress Party's supporters constituted an overt and outspoken general opposition to Muslim newcomers.[8] Despite overt opposition like that exemplified by the Progress Party, Norway has historically provided and continues to provide asylum to a substantial number of Muslim newcomers, particularly relative to the national population. This acceptance is an objective manifestation of relative generosity and is rooted in a dedication to the resettlement of refugees, including those from somewhat contested contexts of origin. In short, the issue of Syria and the contentious politics of refugee migration are salient and actively debated in Norway and, to an extent, are linked with sociocultural concerns—namely religion. As in the case of the Party for Freedom in the Netherlands (see chapter 5), we confront evidence of a gap between overt and covert expressions of tolerance, which indicates that a multilayered view of the xenophobe is worth considering.

As in previous chapters, the approach taken in the Norwegian survey experiment untangled overt from covert forms of antipathy. In addition, the use of distinct frames allowed for the separation of respondents' perceptions of Muslim refugees and other types of Muslim newcomers. As detailed in chapter 2, the survey technique varied the extent to which anonymity was guaranteed, which mitigated possible changes in expression because of anticipated social stigma. The observed differences in response patterns between overt expression and covert expression captured under conditions of absolute and permanent anonymity revealed the extent to which opposition to Muslim newcomers was masked and the extent to which *support* for such newcomers was overstated. To isolate the role of need in determining survey respondents' support for Muslim newcomers, three distinct frames were presented to independent random samples. These frames made explicit the religious dimension of the newcomers but varied the category of need, delineating a general category (i.e., people) from a category defined simply by the newcomers' relationship to the autochthonous population (i.e., immigrants). The latter could have evoked associations with labor-market participation or family ties. The third frame defined Muslim newcomers as qualified refugees, thus linking them to legal definitions of need (e.g., violence, discrimination). Differences in perceptions of Muslim *people*, *immigrants*, and *refugees* were contrasted—in terms of both overt and covert response patterns. The experiment was collected as part of the Norwegian Citizen Panel and was representative of the national adult population in 2016, the year in which data were collected. Some results from this survey experiment, designed in collaboration with Natalia Malancu, were published with Zan Strabac in 2020 (see appendix 5 for a detailed overview of the experimental design).[9]

Table 7.1 offers insight into the sort of welcome different categories of Muslim newcomers to Norway might expect. Broadly, the pattern is one of consistency. The results for overt and covert expression point toward greater support for frames that do not characterize Muslim newcomers as immigrants (i.e., people and refugees). The use of the term *immigrants* resulted in about 7 to 8 percentage points less covertly expressed support for Muslim newcomers than when the terms *people* and *refugees* were used. The category "refugees" elicited comparable support with the category "people": 64 percent and 63 percent, respectively. The implication of this finding is that in Norway, being Muslim and a refugee does not constitute a measurably sympathetic category of need. In other words, the moral connotation inherent in the category of "refugee" does not reduce antipathy relative to more ambiguous designations (e.g., "people"). That said,

TABLE 7.1 SUPPORT FOR MUSLIM PEOPLE, IMMIGRANTS, AND REFUGEES TO LIVE IN NORWAY

			Percentage who mask
	Overt	Covert	(Overt–covert)
People	63%*	40%*	23%*
Immigrants	56%*	33%*	24%*
Refugees	64%*	42%*	22%*

Source: A. Høgestøl and Ø. Skjervheim, Norwegian Citizen Panel 2016, Seventh Wave, https://doi.org/10.18712/NSD-NSD2401-V6.

Note: The overt question was worded as follows: "Should Norway allow people/immigrants/refugees from Muslim countries to come and live here?" The covert questions were worded similarly but administered such that no direct indication of support or opposition was required. (See chapter 2 for a more detailed description of the technique and appendix 5 for the full text of all questions.) In the table, * indicates that the reported percentage was significantly different from zero (p ≤ 0.05).

all frames—people, immigrants, and refugees—garnered overt support from most survey respondents.

Covert support, at least superficially, tells a similar story to that articulated by the overt xenophobe. Describing the newcomers as Muslim immigrants elicited an estimated 8 percentage points less support from the Norwegian public than frames using the terms *people* and *refugees*. This difference is nearly identical to the 7 percent reduction in support recorded for overt support. As with the overt pattern, the level of covert support for Muslim refugees and people was conspicuously similar. Two notable details of this pattern offer some important insight and nuance to the interpretation of the survey findings.

First, the difference between overt and covert expressions of support was large in Norway. About one-quarter of expressed support was found only in overt expression. The strategic response of the xenophobe is to present a welcoming facade. Covert expression, which defines the second layer of the multilayered model of xenophobic expression, suggests a significantly and substantively less supportive context of reception than does overt expression. This finding is in sharp contrast to those of the surveys conducted in the United States and in the pre-Brexit period in the United Kingdom, where antipathy, so long as it was directed at Muslims, resulted in little to no concealment. Antipathy directed at Muslims was similarly expressed by the overt and covert xenophobe in both contexts. Norway, in contrast, offers insight into a context in which opposition that targets Muslims anticipates stigmatization. Those who expressed targeted opposition to Muslim newcomers—whether defined as people, immigrants, or refugees—anticipated stigmatization and adjusted their articulation of opposition accordingly.

Second, the observed strategic masking was similar across the three frames. Despite a clear minority of the Norwegian public were estimated to covertly support the arrival of Muslim newcomers, there is no evidence that refugees elicited greater support than newcomers defined as people or immigrants. This finding matches the pattern observed for overt xenophobia. The assumption that being persecuted for reasons of race, religion, nationality, membership of a particular social group, or political opinion creates a greater moral impetus for support and as a result a more welcoming context of reception does not appear to hold in the case in Norway. Based on the survey results, a Muslim defined simply as a person could expect a welcome similar to that offered to a Muslim defined as a refugee, given the 40 percent and 42 percent of reported covert support for Muslim "people" and "refugees," respectively. The message is clear. Although antipathy is strategically masked, it is substantial, and refugees receive no reprieve.

Although the observed overt and covert pattern in Norway is indicative, few permanent and generalized conclusions should be drawn. This is true for most of the evidence in this book because the key to the multilayered model of xenophobic expression is sensitivity to context, which constantly evolves. The experiment conducted in Norway provides an admittedly limited window into the public perception of refugees because it assessed only one moment and one context. In addition, the frames intentionally focused on Muslim newcomers, which made sense in 2016, but would need to be adapted to consider the distinct reception offered Ukrainians in many contexts of destination after the Russian invasion.

Chapter 4 offered insight into potential differences in overt and covert support for migrants from Eastern Europe and those from Muslim-majority countries to the United Kingdom. Before the Brexit referendum, support for Eastern Europeans was significantly and substantively overstated, particularly among political centrists. The gap between overt and covert sentiment was also much larger than that observed for Muslim migrants, which was attributed to in-group membership in terms of race or ethnicity. However, in the post-Brexit period (about when the Norwegian experiment was fielded), differences in perceptions of Muslim and Eastern European migrants had vanished, and the level of masking was identical. That said, the results of the UK survey experiment are of limited insight here because the question of refugee migration was not included (see appendix 2 for a description of the experimental design of the UK study).

Although it cannot be addressed here, the difference in reception experienced by refugees fleeing the violence in Syria and those fleeing the invasion of Ukraine deserves targeted and sustained attention in the academic literature. It is true that the case of Syria matches the frames described in table 7.1 and until very recently dominated the public's perception of refugee migration to Europe, but this is no longer the case, and a change in context inevitably leads to a change in strategy by the xenophobe. Although the differences are clear in terms of religion and region of origin, there are notable similarities between the two refugee flows. Both countries of origin are situated near the European border, and as a result the bulk of the movement across borders is via European land borders. Ukraine is immediately adjacent to a number of EU states. Similarly, although far from identically situated, Syria abuts the southern border of Turkey—a North Atlantic Treaty Organization (NATO) country that shares a border with two EU states (three if you consider Cyprus, the whole of which is an EU state, although Northern Cyprus has a more complex legal arrangement). Despite these notably limited similarities in terms of geography and the root cause of refugee flows, differences in legal, social, and political reception dominate the debate and therefore the context of reception.

THE NEXUS OF RACE, RELIGION, AND REFUGEE STATUS

The differences in reception between Syrian and Ukrainian asylum seekers and subsequent support for the resulting refugee population are somewhat troubling in that the pattern indicates that other attributes of the potential refugees—most notably ethnicity and religion—create distinct perceptions of acceptability in Europe. No claim for some objective legal standard would be a viable explanation for the observed differences. Other factors rooted in attributes like religion, race, and ethnicity (i.e., sociocultural differences) affect how the need of these newcomers is perceived as deserving in some contexts of reception.

Herein lies the issue. The label "refugee," which character-izes one of the most sympathetic forms of border crossing—reflected in a long-standing and internationally recognized legal framework—is theoretically rooted in a moral imperative. However, deservedness does not translate into acceptance. The evidence from Norway shows that, at least in some interactions, Muslim refugees experience increasingly similar levels of hostil-ity to those directed at nonrefugee immigrant groups. Moreover, the xenophobe systematically elects covert expression in some contexts, which indicates that antipathy toward asylum-based immigration is morally and socially problematic even to those who find antipathy appealing. In other words, overt support can be ephemeral when the covert xenophobe remains unwavering, as was observed before and after the financial crisis in the United States (see chapter 3).

This pernicious and covert opposition could be rooted in an implicitly intersectional perception held of certain groups of refugees. Two salient and overlapping attributes—religion and ethnicity—help explain the absence of greater sympathy directed at some refugee populations relative to others. In the case of arrivals from Muslim-majority countries, assuming successful transit across Turkey in the case of Syrians, the journey to peti-tion for asylum also includes an entrance into a context in which a majority of the population identify as either Christian or, in some cases, express limited interest in a religious affiliation.[10] The result is a clear out-group, which—as we saw in chapter 6—creates a distinct context for xenophobic expression. This conflu-ence of Muslim and refugee statuses creates a context in which there is a tension between a perceived need (i.e., asylum) and a socially distant group-level attribute (i.e., belief in Islam). The result is a greater likelihood that the social stigma of expressed and targeted intolerance toward refugees, driven by moral impetus, will be mitigated by a reduced need to mask intolerance toward a group perceived as relatively distant. As we saw in the case of the United States, support for Muslim and Christian immigrants was expressed overtly in very different ways.

Ethnicity and race are potentially nontrivial contributors to the variations in reception that refugees experience—both covert and overt. The evidence presented in this chapter, which speaks specifically to the reception offered to Muslim refugees in Norway, offers little direct insight into the role of race or ethnicity as an additional frame from the perspective of the potential xenophobe. The differences in the extent to which some European states have supported asylum seekers from Ukraine relative Syria suggests that ethnic differences may play a role in shaping public opinion and public policy. But for the same reason that religion and refugee status intersect, ethnicity is unlikely to be interpreted as construct wholly independent of historical links to contexts of origin and broader notions of in-group identity. The role of out-group differences, whether rooted in ethnicity, religion, refugee status—or all three—is undoubtedly meaningful. As the case of Norway highlights, refugees are not placed in a singular and welcoming category of need. The legal and definitional approach toward defining a refugee has its limits, which the clear divergence in reception between Syrian and Ukrainian refugees makes clear.

This divergence could be evidence that refugees are perceived as little different from migrants by some. As the pattern in Norway indicates, even under conditions of anonymity, there appears to be little unique sympathy directed toward Muslim refugees. Moreover, in this case, the deservedness (i.e., category of need) associated with refugees could create a larger divergence between the prevalence of overt and covert xenophobia. That said, in contexts or situations in which there is a greater

anticipated stigma for expressing opposition to refugee migration (either overall or toward a target group), the xenophobe,
via a strategy of stigma avoidance, could easily contribute to a
misperception that refugees are more sympathetically viewed by
the general public. As with the pattern observed for race in some
contexts (see chapter 5), opposing a group legally or politically
deemed deserving of shelter can incur costs that would inhibit
the overt expression of antipathy. In this way, despite the pattern seen in Norway, it is entirely plausible that some contexts
or groups (e.g., non-Muslim migrants) would encounter a larger
and targeted gap between overt and covert sentiment. What is
clear from the evidence presented here, given the rapidly shifting landscape and scale of refugee migration flows to Europe
and the United States, generalizations about the specific attitudes prevalent in a context of reception and the attitudinal
behavior of the associated xenophobe are of limited value.

As with other examples of strategic xenophobic expression,
significant and targeted masking has implications for anonymous behavior, suggesting the clear utility of activating (even
indirectly) refugee-based opposition as a means of generating
a political constituency or other interest-based movement. This
strategic activation is an observed component of the populist political playbook, as was the case with the 2020 exit of the
Progress Party from government in Norway. The case study in
this chapter indicates that one can suggest, sometimes using
very subtle cues, opposition to refugee migration or migration
overall and—at least in some contexts—placate or energize
a sizable constituency. In addition, the level of masking indicates that opposition is substantially larger when anonymity
is offered as an outlet (e.g., via voting). Antirefugee sentiment
and anti-immigrant sentiment are potentially two sides of the
same coin. Either is a plausible vote-getter to a percentage of the

constituency that is notably larger than a straightforward opinion poll would indicate. As was discussed in chapter 3, populist anti-immigrant political rhetoric is a public manifestation of preferences that voters might express when anonymity can be preserved. As such, it would be foolhardy to consider a category of need—of which the refugee is clearly deserving—to offer protection, in any meaningful sense, from the animosity the xenophobe directs at other categories of newcomers.

Overall, this chapter offers an admittedly narrow overview of the perception of refugees in the eyes of the xenophobe. Although the data collection was limited to a single case study, the findings illuminate the drawbacks of having so little empirical evidence of covert attitudes toward refugee migrants. It is not easy to dismiss the insight of Norway, nor is it reasonable to consider it sufficient. There is clear evidence of voting and legal patterns that treat distinct asylum seekers very differently depending on the context of origin. Refugee flows are likely to remain a salient dimension of migration overall and as a result to remain a target of the xenophobe's ire. Based at least in the case study described here, refugees cannot expect a warmer reception than other migrants. In fact, asylum seekers can confront a substantial level of masked antipathy upon arrival. As we've seen with religion, race, and ethnicity, the xenophobe's strategy of expression is very reactive to context and interaction.

Because the face of refugee migration is continuously shifting— the emergence of Ukraine as a dominant context of origin in a matter of months is a case in point—there are likely to be numerous circumstances in which the Norwegian lack of distinction between Muslim refugees and Muslim newcomers will not repeat itself. Understanding how a definitional approach to anticipating the reception of refugees, in which one either qualifies or does not qualify as a refugee, does not and will not work if the goal is to truly anticipate and understand the xenophobe. It is possible that some new arrivals will be put in unique categories of need and that in these instances, that placement would supersede the xenophobe's gravitation toward overt antipathy. However, it is more likely that we will only know with any confidence if this is indeed the case if the possibility of strategic masking can be mitigated.

CONCLUSION

Multiple Layers, Legal Remedies, Anonymous Acts

WHAT TO DO WITH A MULTILAYERED MODEL OF THE XENOPHOBE

An understanding of the *other*, whether based on experience or preexisting stereotypes, is an inherent dimension of any social interaction. As a result, the multilayered model of the xenophobe need not be limited to those who direct their ire at migrants, the object of interest in this book. The focus here on how the xenophobe finds expression is not an accident. The perception of people who cross a border and enter a new context provides an intuitive place to engage with the meaning and interpretation of the stranger. As mentioned in the first paragraph of the first chapter, understanding the xenophobe requires a careful consideration of the fearful and the feared. When this archetypal other is a complete stranger, judgments are fundamentally shaped by contextual rules because no other information is available. These rules are governed by the anticipation of stigma—or lack thereof. The expectation of social and sometimes legal consequences results in the xenophobe electing strategically opportune pathways of expression. These strategic pathways evolve along with the social context within which the xenophobe navigates.

The empirical evidence that formed the backbone of this book was derived from many frames and contexts of reception. The result has been an expansive and clear picture that has dispelled any notion that the xenophobe is a fixed entity, driven by mechanisms that are interpretable in all situations. This view is no longer tenable, and the emergent multilayered view of the xenophobe underscores just how significant an insight this is.

Let's start with materialist models of the xenophobe. Rooted in the view that newcomers are perceived as competition for employment or wages, materialist concerns are both frequently critiqued and remarkably resilient, retaining a position of legitimacy as a key explanation of animosity toward migrants and migration. The logic is impersonal and as such appealing. Opposition is not about anything inherent in the targeted individual or group but instead rests on an appearance of objectivity that the presence of new workers will have negative implications for nationally defined economic opportunities that, in the eyes of some, should be reserved for those who arrived first. The materialist perspective, captured by a "lifeboat is full" view of the economy, is rarely far from any effort to understand why it is that newcomers are unwelcome, particularly during moments of economic hardship. However, a multilayered model of the xenophobe questions the generalizability (or even applicability) of a materialist perspective in many circumstances. The evidence shown here supports a very different interpretation. Materialist concerns are better understood as a pathway by which socially and culturally rooted opposition can be destigmatized. This approach paints quite a different picture of the public-facing xenophobe. And more importantly, it reveals that the private, covert xenophobe—shrouded in anonymity—expresses much greater antipathy overall and, in some cases, very few preferences in terms of the attributes of the other that are targeted.

This perspective is a meaningful shift in our understanding of what constitutes a xenophobe and xenophobia. It moves away from a hunt for mechanisms in an absolute sense and turns toward how intolerance is regulated and articulated. Material concerns, at least in some circumstances (e.g., the recent financial crisis in the United States), provide an excuse rather than a motive.

Materialist explanations are not the only perspective a multi-layered model questions. Let's also consider the roles of religion, race, and ethnicity in the expression of xenophobic sentiment. The key question is about the extent to which racists and Islamophobes should be considered distinct from those who oppose the generalized other, regardless of the out-group differences used to frame the opposition. In short, is an Islamophobe somehow more tolerant toward newcomers of religions other than Islam? Similarly, is opposition greater when the targets are migrants who are racially or ethnically different from the xenophobe? Answering these questions can offer insight into bridges between often rigidly and, I would argue, arbitrarily demarcated forms of prejudice. As emphasized from the start, the effort here is to better understand the nuance of prejudice. This consideration of the xenophobe as a subject of study defined by situationally determined norms does not minimize the role or impact of meaningful forms of pervasive and pernicious bigotry rooted in religious, racial, and ethnic intolerance. Instead, exploring commonalities in consciously masked intolerance is an important addition to existing perspectives on unconscious forms bigotry such as color-blind racism. Here is why.

Time and time again an anticipation of social stigma when expressing intolerance translates into strategic outcomes that are categorized into overt and covert forms of expression. Our presentation of our views is selective because our goal is to shape how we are viewed by others. We manage this process—the best we can—which is an intentional and conscious act. In other words, we know very well how others see us (or at least we think we do), and we work hard to manage those impressions. The xenophobe is no different, and the evidence in this book shows how the xenophobe systematically alters the extent to which they target certain groups overtly and others covertly. What the multilayered model highlights are clear commonalities among distinct forms of xenophobia that emerge only when the context of expression offers protection from the possibility of stigmatization. In covert interactions, Muslims find little difference in terms of reception, whereas other religious groups receive overt preferential treatment. In short, the Islamophobe is a public actor. The xenophobe is less so.

A multilayered model also offers a way to account for the strategic and intentional masking of race-based prejudice. Racism and ethnocentrism are similarly shaped by the context in which they are expressed. One way to think about this phenomenon, which helps underscore the divergence from discriminatory attitudes perpetuated via unconscious biases, is that the stigmatization of racism can have the unintended consequence of pushing it underground, which limits its presence in the expression of the overt xenophobe. This understanding is quite different from one that interprets a change in the prevalence of the xenophobe in an absolute sense. Creating contexts in which it is frowned upon and, in some instances, legally prohibited to express racist or ethnocentric views might also result in a reduction in overt xenophobia—whether it be rooted in racism or ethnocentrism. A multilayered model accounts for the fact that intolerance can be intentionally and consciously masked, which provides a different perspective from one in which racism and ethnocentrism are thought to be meaningfully absent from the hearts and minds of society. Importantly, there is no need to assume that that the perpetuation of observable inequalities in contexts with limited overt intolerance is attributable to the effect of unconscious biases. Instead, the multilayered model allows for an understanding that masked biases, which are very much conscious and intentional, are a demonstrable repository of intolerance.

As we saw in Ireland and the Netherlands, race can appear to play only a minor role in overt expressions of intolerance, which is the outermost layer of the multilayered xenophobe. It is only when anonymity alleviates the need to strategically avoid stigmatization that we see real variation between distinct outgroups. There is an undeniable norm in some contexts to be tolerant toward racial in-groups with an equally notable overreporting of tolerance toward migrants of a race different from that of the majority. Race matters, but its implications in terms of reception for newcomers is obfuscated when the xenophobe is taken at face value. Moreover, it was found that respondents of one ethnic group (e.g., Hispanics in the United States) expressed about the same level of overt and covert opposition to closing the U.S. border, meaning they engaged in no strategic masking, whereas a significant and substantive gap was found between overt and covert opposition among Black and White respondents. Race and ethnicity are meaningful for those expressing sentiment toward newcomers and for those on the receiving end.

A multilayered perspective injects a much-needed dose of skepticism into the conversation. Overt expression can be understood as impactful and interpretable but, at the same time, limited in its ability to capture the xenophobe in any meaningful way. Similarly, unconsciously held forms of intolerance, which can be overtly denied, are theoretically and operationally separated from intentional, strategic, and consciously masked sentiment. This understanding questions several key assumptions that we often make about the prevalence of and motive for attitudes toward newcomers—both negative and positive. For example, materialist concerns are less stigmatized than those over race or ethnicity, but that does not mean that they are a core determinant of intolerance. Similarly, race can be de-emphasized, but contexts in which it is do not point toward a postracial society because intentional masking continues to exist. Also, Islamophobes are demonstrably emboldened by a reduction in social stigma. If we focus on the greater overt expression of intolerance that results, we might be led to believe that other migrant communities experience a warm(er) reception in all domains. The covert layer of xenophobic expression points out how wrong that interpretation can be because evidence has shown that other migrant groups are seen far less favorably when sentiment is masked. If there is one message to take from this book, let it be the following: ignoring the strategically masked xenophobe makes us complicit in the intended deception.

LEGAL REMEDIES (OR THEIR ABSENCE) AND THE EMERGENCE OF SOCIAL STIGMA

Legislating overt intolerance is widely practiced, which has implications for covert expression. Hate speech and efforts to reduce it are common, although it is difficult to define and target for interdiction. Without debating whether the legal regulation of speech is a useful exercise or ethical approach, it is undeniable that such efforts have been made. The most widely cited legislation in this area is Article 20 of the International Covenant on Civil and Political Rights, which was adopted by the United Nations on December 16, 1966.[1] This article has been adapted in some form, often with conditions, throughout much of the world. Many countries have gone beyond the covenant to offer a more expansive protection from intolerance (e.g., Ireland), whereas others have placed conditions on its ratification (e.g., the United States). That said, many legal contexts have pursued some form of legislative remedy to deal with targeted expressions of intolerance.

Let's take the case of the Netherlands. Going as far back as 1978, the Netherlands enacted legal sanctioning for the distribution of propaganda that called for racial homogeneity and the removal of guestworkers—specifically, migrants from Turkey and Suriname.[2] Fast-forward about thirty years, and we see that efforts to curb hate speech remained a common but not always effective tool. Most notably was the case against the controversial yet successful politician Geert Wilders for inciting hate toward Muslims in 2010 and 2011. Of note, Wilders was acquitted. The point being here that efforts to legislate hate are uneven but certainly far from unknown.

Ireland recently sought to assess the scope and effectiveness of hate speech legislation with a public consultation and formal report published in 2020.[3] Ireland is a signatory to the International Covenant on Civil and Political Rights with some conditions, but the more relevant legislative basis for its efforts to combat hate speech is the 1989 Prohibition of Incitement to Hatred Act.[4] That said, the legislation has rarely, if ever, been used. What is notable is not the effectiveness of efforts to legally sanction hate speech but the prevalence of such initiatives. These efforts will surely be tested if emergent political movements like Ireland First, which uses strategic masking,[5] find success in the future.

It is here that I will make a somewhat controversial point. Imposing legal limits on overt expressions of targeted intolerance is an explicit effort to increase the stigma of such sentiment. If the results of the list experiments conducted for this book are to be believed, this strategy does not result in some absolute reduction in the prevalence of xenophobia. Instead, targeting overt expression can result in the strategic use of masked forms of expression. In other words, making it illegal to be a racist can result in the racist moving underground. As will be discussed in a moment, this strategic move has real implications for behavior. This is not to say that overtly xenophobic rhetoric should be left unaddressed. To the contrary. Instead, a reasonable takeaway from the evidence presented in this book is that the multilayered model of the xenophobe indicates that placing restrictions on overt expressions of intolerance are useful only on the outermost layer of xenophobic expression. As such, they are limited in scope and efficacy.

Unfortunately, addressing strategically masked forms of intolerance is rarely straightforward. One approach is to consider observable outcomes of meaning that are more structural; for example, differences in emergency service response times based on certain characteristics of the caller, differences in the likelihood that public defenders will advocate for certain types of legal sanctions based on the race or ethnicity of the defendant, and variations in the process of naturalization or the granting of asylum based on the applicant's country of origin. Different outcomes in such situations indicate systematic differences in preferences and attitudes. Greater scrutiny can force the aggregate outcome toward greater public exposure and increase the likelihood that social stigma might be expected—at least at some stage in the process. The idea is to create transparency and move known areas of discrimination away from contexts in which stigma can be avoided. The key mechanism for regulating xenophobia is social stigma, which needs transparency to be applicable.

Perhaps not all concerns raised by a multilayered view of the xenophobe are resolvable via public policy or social or political intervention. The reality, as evidenced here is that the xenophobe inhabits distinct layers depending on context. This understanding means that xenophobia may be less manageable than originally believed because attitudinal expression can no longer be taken at face value. This finding should not be interpreted as giving up. It remains true that the xenophobe is relevant and of concern even in contexts in which there is little acceptability of intolerance in the public domain. In a sense, a multilayered perspective is a validation of the experience of those who find direct measures of public opinion or soapbox-level political discourse disingenuous. Such experience doesn't mean that the overt xenophobe is irrelevant, but the evidence provided here points to the importance of seeing overt intolerance as only one aspect of a much more complicated and situationally specific object of study. The key is to understand that there is no generalizable, stable, and objective view of the xenophobe. Instead, each layer, in some contexts, *is* the xenophobe. Taking this nuanced understanding of who the xenophobe is prevents counterproductive debates about determinants of intolerance—in some absolute sense—from becoming the focus of the conversation.

THE MANY CONTEXTS OF EXPRESSION: DISTINGUISHING THE OVERT FROM THE COVERT

Social science has long tried to link intentions and behavior.[6] One obvious limitation in the experiments conducted for this book, which aimed to define and test a multilayered model of the xenophobe, is that they offer only attitudinal evidence. Attitudes might show intent, but that is not the same as observing the impact of a behavioral outcome. This limitation is not unique to assessments of intolerance and is in fact a consistent—and well-founded—critique of attitudinal measures as useful predictors of behavior in general.[7] Although all methodological problems cannot be resolved at once, a multilayered perspective does propose a new—and somewhat radical—theoretical avenue to pursue. Covert sentiment, particularly that which is intentionally masked, has a lot in common with covert acts.

Figure con.1 makes this distinct link between covert attitudes and acts clear. Nestled between overtly and unconsciously held attitudes, the second layer is defined by a key mechanism: intentionality. The crucial requirement for expression at this layer is access to anonymity, by which the stigma of intolerance can be mitigated or wholly avoided. It follows that the same xenophobe who would find the expression of intolerance to necessitate masking would also find that xenophobic acts worth strategically avoiding in contexts and interactions in which stigmatization would be anticipated. Expression at this layer is thus very different from that at the first and third layers, which does not entail any intentional masking (although at the third layer, intolerance is masked even from the xenophobe themselves, constituting a form of self-deception).

To highlight how covert acts are limited to the second layer of the multilayered model, let's consider the other layers. The first layer, defined by overt expression, aligns open expression with a near absence of any anticipated social stigma. This is a freedom to act on intolerance and indicates how the overt xenophobe can be more impactful on the day-to-day lives of those targeted. If nothing is masked, intolerance would form part of many direct interactions. Of course, the reality is not so simply delineated. There might be exceptional circumstances in which saying something and doing something might substantively deviate to the extent that behavior is subject to social pressures

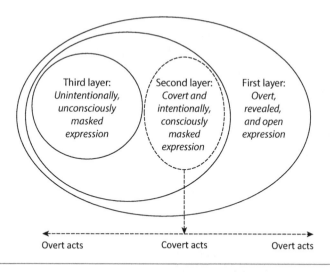

Overt acts   Covert acts   Overt acts

FIGURE C.1 The relationship between the multilayered model of
xenophobic expression and behavior

that attitudes are not. As figure con.1 indicates, the theoretical
link among the layers of xenophobic expression and the extent to
which behavior (i.e., acts) is overt or covert is a spectrum, not a
light switch. The crucial difference among the layers is that strategically masked sentiment, which is by definition reactive to
social stigmatization, is present only in the second layer. This
strategic response is theoretically the largest determinant of
anonymous behavior.

Relative to the first layer, the link between the third, unconscious layer of xenophobic expression and behavior is somewhat
more complex. Although an assessment of unconscious bias was
outside the empirical scope of the evidence presented in this
book, unconscious expression deserves mention, too, because
it constitutes a distinct layer of the xenophobe. This layer also
involves a degree of deception, albeit self-deception. Simply put,

unconsciously masked attitudes, which are overtly denied, should not result in any theoretical expectation that related intolerances will be strategically hidden. To the contrary, the absence of self-awareness results in a theoretical expectation that overtly intolerant acts would be easily observable, just not interpreted as resting on an intolerant or xenophobic foundation by the perpetrator. As the individual is unaware of the presence of prejudice, behavioral outcomes are similarly interpreted to be free of bias. This chain of logic in a sense provides the link between unconscious forms of intolerance and observed, structural patterns of discrimination. When considering race, the rhetoric of tolerance by those who can be empirically linked to patterns of intolerance is at the root of the argument for color-blind racism. From this admittedly abstract theoretical premise, there are some straightforward examples to consider.

To underscore the potential link between intentionally masked intolerance and behavior, let's start with voting. In the case of the Netherlands, the context of the survey experiments described in chapter 5, the period during which we observed a sizable gap between overtly and covertly expressed tolerance was also one in which there was demonstrable electoral success for the Party for Freedom, led by Geert Wilders, who was once prosecuted for hate speech. This party received a substantial share of the vote, although overt public opinion suggested that anti-immigrant sentiment should not have appealed to the majority of the population. An understanding of this outcome based only on overt expression is incomplete at best. Instead, it is not at all strange that voting would deviate from what can be overtly observed. From Goffman's perspective, voting is an obviously discreditable act. In a sense, eliminating the potential social consequences of the act of voting is the very reason that the secret ballot is a fundamental component of an open and free democratic system. It is also why dog whistling can be effective. If a candidate can avoid social and political stigmatization while simultaneously signaling support for perspectives that are intentionally masked (i.e., via the second layer), the result could be a substantive electoral advantage because the process of anonymous voting allows those who want to avoid appearing to be in favor of a stigmatized candidate to support the same candidate as the those who are openly bigoted.

The example of Brexit offered in chapters 4 and 6 provides a similar insight into the link between masked intolerance and behavioral outcomes. In the case of Brexit, the gap between overt and covert sentiment increased among right-leaning survey respondents after the vote in favor of the United Kingdom leaving the United Kingdom. The results of the experiments indicate that social contexts can change quickly and that these changes affect different segments of the electorate to varying degrees. Voting behavior, an inherently anonymous act, can be anticipated better if one considers it to be linked more closely with anonymous attitudes—rather than considering direct polling to be insightful for divisive topics. On the flip side, it would be reasonable to think that there might be less of an expectation of overt intolerance being palatable in the public sphere. A multilayered perspective avoids the naive narrative that xenophobia has become mainstream or that the xenophobe is on retreat. It is not that simple. Instead, a theoretical expectation from the model introduced here is that covert acts reflect the strategic preferences of the xenophobe and that covert acts are inevitably less affected by stigmatization. This is where the contradiction emerges between contextual limits on overt intolerance and simultaneously observed increases in the success of populist political and social movements that target migrants, among other out-groups.

Intervening in the process of voting to mitigate the influence of the xenophobe is unlikely to be desirable even if it were feasible. Instead, the lesson here is that it is worthwhile, when relevant, to highlight a link between seemingly benign or stigma-free calls for intolerance (e.g., materialist narratives in campaign rhetoric) and the broader appeal of sociocultural forms of xenophobia, which are far more likely to garner social stigma. This is the lesson—to the extent that one can be learned—from the Brexit campaign. In that case, the veiled foregrounding of concerns about certain countries of origin (e.g., Turkey) and certain types of migrants (e.g., refugees from Muslim-majority countries) did not clearly overlap with concepts like racism and Islamophobia—at least in the minds of some more centrist voters. Those motivated by sociocultural concerns got the message without needing to be rallied to an explicit call for racist, ethnocentric, or Islamophobic support. Instead, the message was more implicit and as such resulted in a broader coalition of support. To address this form of dog whistling, it is useful to make the link between a subtle pattern of covert suggestion—rather than overt articulation—as indicative of outreach to those who would be attracted to types of xenophobia that are abhorrent to the mainstream electorate.

It is worth remembering that making explicit the link between destigmatized intolerance and the strategic masking of intolerance, assuming that is a reasonable connection to make, creates a context in which there might be an even greater obfuscation of intolerance. Candidates who intend to benefit from the xenophobe's support might just further strategically mask their support for related policies. The dog whistle would just get fainter. However, it is also plausible that pointing out links in terms of rhetoric and appeals to xenophobic support for candidates that are being simultaneously evaluated on other issues might be effective. Although estimates of covert intolerance in the survey results were often greater than those of overt intolerance, covert intolerance was not always a clear majority, and large constituencies (e.g., in Norway) remained unmotivated by appeals to xenophobia. It follows that a cleavage between the xenophobe and mainstream politics would bring the normative pressure of social stigma into the political arena. This was the process used to push overtly racist sentiment out of the political mainstream in contexts that historically embraced such intolerances, as reflected in the perpetration of colonialism and slavery.

Aside from voting, hiring is another area that is theoretically more sensitive to strategically masked intolerance. As with voting, hiring offers a breadth of criteria by which candidates can plausibly be evaluated. These criteria provide opportunities for discrimination, which, like responses to a list experiment, can be decoupled from any explicit manifestation of bias. Correspondence studies, which are the mainstay of research into discrimination in hiring, intentionally manipulate candidate characteristics such that employers receive near-identical résumés, the only difference being an attribute that could be covertly targeted (e.g., migrant status, race, ethnicity, gender). The evidence from such studies consistently shows that these attributes do factor into hiring decisions—or at least in the rate at which recontacts are made or requests for interviews result for applicants with certain attributes.[8] That said, it is very unlikely that direct queries would reveal such preferences on the part of those who hire. A better approach, as with predicting more extreme voting preferences, is to consider overt sentiment to be limited in its ability to dictate covert behavior. Although eliminating anonymity is not straightforward or, in many cases, even desirable (e.g., voting), hiring is a different matter. In the case of employment, the shift of discriminatory preferences toward the second layer of the multilayered model implies that making the process of hiring more transparent might reduce the extent to which prejudicial outcomes can avoid stigmatization. Although intolerant sentiment is often easily masked, some areas of behavior could be removed from the realm of anonymity, and hiring is a good candidate.

Anonymity and its role in job candidate evaluation have been explored in several ways, but the typical approach is to reduce the bias that unconscious preferences introduce into the hiring process by removing identifying information from candidates' applications. The result, in theory, is an inability to act prejudicially on biases—known or unknown—because key information about particular attributes (e.g., class, race, ethnicity, gender) cannot be identified by those in a position to hire. This is a useful approach for addressing the third layer of the xenophobe and, in some instances, may even help deceive those who would mask discriminatory tendencies when justifying their hiring preferences. However, this type of anonymity does not address the fundamental mechanism that results in masking being a useful strategy to begin with. A better approach is to make the hiring criteria and decision-making process as transparent and accurately documented as possible.[9] This approach, rather than a focus on anonymizing applicant details, aids efforts to link the hiring process with interactions that require overt expression.

The core takeaway is that the systematic expansion of transparency—anonymity's antimatter—can reduce the number of acts that can be pursued by the covert xenophobe. This approach seeks to decouple the link between anonymous expression and anonymous acts. In the cases of voting and hiring, the theoretical expectation that intolerance will become a tangible act when stigma can be avoided is an obvious extension of the evidence provided in these pages that links anonymity to covertly expressed intolerance. These are just two examples, and the suggested intervention is somewhat limited. For instance, greater scrutiny of the act of voting would not be a reasonable or desirable remedy. A coherent operationalization would need to be context specific by reflecting the legal, bureaucratic, and sociocultural contexts in which an act takes place. That said, the intentional use of social stigma as a mechanism to limit the xenophobe's ability to act on their preferences is a meaningful translation of the results from this book into behaviorally oriented solutions. An understanding of the layers of the xenophobe can inform some interventions that directly confront the otherwise obscured reality and mechanism (i.e., stigma) that undergird covert sentiment.

THE FUTURE OF THE XENOPHOBE

This book offers a succinct argument for the importance of understanding xenophobic expression via a multilayered model. Each chapter provides evidence of how strategic masking defines some of the most controversial social and political tendencies we confront (e.g., populism, racism, Islamophobia, refugee migration). In each case, the multilayered model of the xenophobe offers a clear accounting of the core theoretical, context-specific mechanism that make certain types of sentiment strategically preferable. An understanding of the key role of social stigma underscores the reality that the type of xenophobe who intentionally and strategically masks their views is far more prevalent than overt expression might lead us to believe. This book provides empirical evidence for a multitude of factors (e.g., economic crises; elite political discourse; racial, ethnic, or religious in-group preferences) that fundamentally shape which forms of xenophobic expression are—and are not—subject to stigmatization. But this evidence provides only a snapshot of the recent past. The multilayered model offers a theoretical anchor. What does the future hold?

One thing is certain. The xenophobe will not seek expression in the future in the same way as has been observed in the recent past. Because the anticipation of social stigma is specific to a particular place and time, an understanding of the evolution of the xenophobe is tied to a longer-term view of changes in the norms governing the context within which intolerance is expressed. As has been shown in the cases of the financial crisis in the United States and the Brexit vote in the United Kingdom, top-down factors can rapidly alter social, economic, and political contexts, which quickly affects the strategy of expression pursued by the xenophobe. As a result, the future is likely to depend on the extent to which openly expressed prejudicial attitudes are tolerated and the space available for anonymous forms of expression and behavior.

In contexts in which intolerant sentiment is trending toward the mainstream, the xenophobe can be expected to anticipate less social stigma, which will result in a more openly hostile reception for newcomers. Such contexts would, in theory, also provide more space for overtly sheltered groups (e.g., co-religionists) to converge with those who are already openly opposed (e.g., Muslims in non-Muslim contexts of reception). In the case of the United States described in this book, the result would be a convergence between overt and covert antipathy expressed toward Muslim and Christian legal migrants. Currently, only covert expression reveals parity in levels of opposition. In contexts in which overtly expressed intolerance deviates from the mainstream, the xenophobe would increasingly anticipate social stigma and strategically opt for covert expression. This choice, as mentioned, is also a potential unintended consequence of efforts to confront the overt xenophobe. Put another way, attempts to highlight links between xenophobic expression and targeted forms of prejudice (e.g., racism, Islamophobia) can, counterintuitively, contribute to the concealment of anti-immigrant sentiment because of an increased anticipation that open intolerant expression will be stigmatized.

The evidence presented in this book suggests an ambitious agenda for future work in two complementary directions. First, the context of reception is not defined only by those who see themselves as recipients. This work, with good reason, focuses on the xenophobe as an independent object of study. This is the start, not the end. As has been welcomed in recent efforts to understand migration more broadly, the implications of strategically masked xenophobia for newcomers are being examined. Just as an understanding of the variation in how the xenophobe seeks expression is insightful, a delineation of the experience of xenophobia between overt acts or sentiment and covert acts or sentiment provides critical insight. As this concluding chapter suggests, some acts (e.g., hiring, voting) are well suited to the covert xenophobe and have real implications for migrants. That said, this view—as opposed to that focused on macro and micro forms of overt intolerance—demands engagement in future research with the migrant experience.

Second, the process by which social stigma emerges is not obvious. As a key mechanism determining the extent to which the xenophobe seeks overt expression, it is crucial that we understand the context-specific process by which the social acceptability of intolerance rises and falls. This process is different from measuring the extent to which intolerance is masked. Instead, research is needed on the emergence, maintenance, and interpretation of social stigma. There is a lot of work on stigma that considers the implications of being stigmatized,[10] but this does not provide insight into what makes a behavior or expression elicit social stigma to begin with. In other words, why different contexts result in different degrees of anticipated stigma remains a mostly unanswered question.

This book offers an unmasking of the xenophobe. We know that the world is ever more mobile. The arrival of newcomers and the perception of this mobility by individuals, groups, societies, and countries will increasingly define many facets of contemporary life. Between patterns of urbanization, refugee migration, environmental displacement, economic shocks, and populist political movements, the migrant will face complex and varied contexts of reception. If a more tolerant and overtly welcoming future is desirable, there is much reason for optimism. We now have a more nuanced and realistic understanding of the motives and behavior of xenophobic expression. We can move beyond self-defeating grand theories that seek to define—once and for all—the fundamental determinants of intolerance. Instead, we can engage with a more agile and flexible perspective that focuses on specific contexts and situations. With clarity about how social stigma arises and is interpreted, we can better understand society's ability to shape how intolerance is expressed. We also can be aware that some layers of the xenophobe are difficult to confront—if they can be confronted at all. The future is not predictable, but an understanding that the xenophobe is multilayered and contextually defined will empower those who prefer tolerance and acceptance. Work in these areas may help prevent the strategic decoupling of deceptive rhetoric like economic necessity from that tied to racial, ethnic, and religious intolerance. Covert patterns can clearly link the two. We can now evaluate the xenophobe's overt presentation with informed skepticism, noting that it is only one act performed for a specific audience.

APPENDIX 1

CHAPTER 3 SURVEY EXPERIMENT: THE UNITED STATES BEFORE AND AFTER THE FINANCIAL CRISIS

The results of the survey experiment described in chapter 3 are derived from two independent data collections in the United States. The first was conducted in 2005,[1] and the results were published via peer review in 2010.[2] The surveys were conducted by phone from a sample of phone numbers drawn using random-digit dialing. For the follow-up, conducted in 2010,[3] some results of which were published via peer review in 2015,[4] surveys were conducted via an online panel. All study collaborators are mentioned in chapter 3. The ability to compare the two samples across time has been covered in detail elsewhere.[5] Both survey experiments were part of a project developed to facilitate access to representative panels and implement experimental designs in the United States called Time-Sharing Experiments for the Social Sciences, funded by the National Science Foundation.

Figure ap.1 shows the design of the list experiment used in the chapter 3 survey experiment. The difference between the total sample size for the 2010 survey experiment and the number of participants in the treatment and control groups is attributable to additional experimental groups having been included in the initial sample that were not used in the experiment about attitudes toward a closed border.

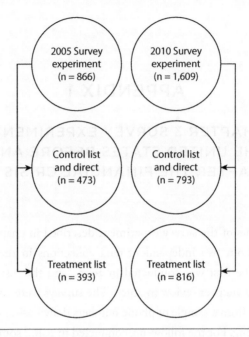

FIGURE AP.1 Design of the chapter 3 survey experiment conducted in the United States

From an initial random sample, two random subsamples—treatment and control—were drawn. The control samples in 2005 and 2010 were given the following list question:

Below you will read three things that sometimes people oppose or are against. After you read all three, just tell us HOW MANY of them you OPPOSE. We do not want to know which ones, just HOW MANY.

(1) The federal government increasing assistance to the poor
(2) Professional athletes making millions of dollars per year
(3) Large corporations polluting the environment

After the list question, the control samples were given the following direct question:

Do you support or oppose cutting off all immigration to the U.S.?

The treatment samples were given the same list question but with four items listed instead of three. The additional focal item was worded as follows:

(4) Cutting off all immigration to the U.S.

A number of concise overviews of the design, implementation, and analysis of a list experiment have been published.[6] The intuition was as follows. The control list provided an average response to the three items and all related measures of central tendency (e.g., mean, standard deviation). These results can be compared to those of the treatment list, which also offered an average response to the items. Because the treatment list included one additional item but differed in no other way, the difference in the mean response between the control and treatment groups provides an estimate of the proportion of participants who agreed with the additional list item. In this case, that was support for a closed U.S. border. To ascertain the proportion who reported their support only via the anonymity of the list experiment, the estimated proportion (derived from the difference between the mean of the control list and the mean of the treatment list) can be compared to the proportion measured via the direct question. As a result, the experimental design allowed for an estimate of overt sentiment, covert sentiment, and the difference between the two.

APPENDIX 2

CHAPTERS 4 AND 6 SURVEY EXPERIMENTS: THE UNITED KINGDOM BEFORE AND AFTER THE BREXIT REFERENDUM

The UK survey experiments described in chapters 4 and 6 were conducted via a longitudinal data collection. The same panel was used for both the pre-Brexit and post-Brexit experiments. The sample was drawn from a larger survey panel in the United Kingdom called the Innovation Panel, which had a clustered, stratified, and equal probability design. The mode of data collection varied. First, respondents were asked to complete an online survey. Second, those who did not complete the survey were recontacted and invited to take part in an in-person interview. For those still unable to be interviewed, a telephone option was offered. The experiments were designed in 2015, and some results were published via peer review in 2021.[1] All study collaborators are mentioned in chapters 4 and 6. Of note, the date and outcome of the Brexit referendum were not known at the time of the experiment's design or by the completion of fieldwork in 2015.

Figure ap.2 shows the design of the two list experiments that measured covert and overt attitudes toward immigration to the United Kingdom before and after the Brexit referendum. Because the study design was longitudinal, the initial sample comprised the same respondents in 2015 and 2016. The longitudinal design also explains the small difference in sample size (n)

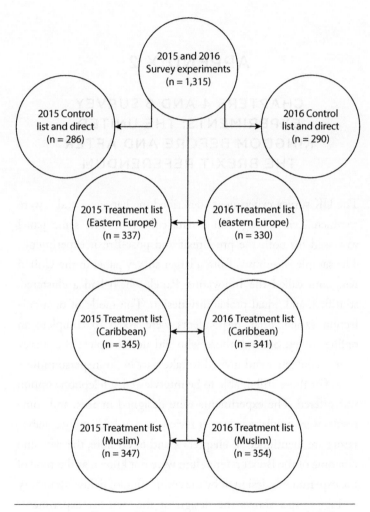

FIGURE AP.2 Design of the chapter 4 survey experiment conducted in the United Kingdom

between the 2015 and 2016 experimental groups. The randomization process was repeated so that respondents were not automatically asked the same questions in each wave.

In each experiment, from an initial random sample, four random subsamples—three treatments and one control—were drawn. The control samples in 2015 and 2016 were given the following list question:

> Of the following three statements, HOW MANY of them do you AGREE with? We don't want to know which statements, just HOW MANY.

(1) The UK should increase assistance to the poor.
(2) The UK should decrease the tax on diesel and petrol.
(3) The UK should allow large corporations to pollute the environment.

After the list question, the control samples were given one of the following three direct questions:

> Do you think the UK should allow people from Eastern European countries to come and live here?
> Do you think the UK should allow people from Caribbean countries to come and live here?
> Do you think the UK should allow people from Muslim countries to come and live here?

The treatment samples were given the same list question but with four items listed instead of three. The additional focal item was worded in one of the following ways:

(4) The UK should allow people from Eastern European countries to come and live here.

(4) The UK should allow people from Caribbean countries to come and live here.

(4) The UK should allow people from Muslim countries to come and live here.

Appendix 1 and chapter 2 provide descriptions of the intuition of the list experiment. The only additional unique feature of this experiment is the multiple treatment groups used. Notably, the treatment samples were independent, meaning that respondents were only asked one of the list questions. This avoided repetition, which further reduced the likelihood that the focal item would be identified. Aside from the use of multiple treatment groups, the implementation of the experiment and the subsequent analysis were consistent with any standard list experiment, resulting in estimates of covert sentiment, overt sentiment, and the difference between the two.

APPENDIX 3

CHAPTER 5 SURVEY EXPERIMENTS: RACE AND ETHNICITY IN IRELAND AND THE NETHERLANDS

The survey experiments described in chapter 5 were conducted in Ireland and the Netherlands. In Ireland, data for the survey experiment were collected from the Economic Sentiment Monitor (ESM), which involved repeated cross-sectional data collection carried out by the Economic and Social Research Institute in Dublin.[1] The ESM was a telephone survey that used post-stratification, within-household weights derived from the Irish Labour Force Survey[2] to guarantee a representative sample of the Irish population. The experiment was fielded in 2017, and some results were published via peer review in 2020 and 2022.[3] All study collaborators are mentioned in chapter 5.

Figure ap.3 shows the design of the list experiment conducted in Ireland. The study targeted the intersection of race and migration by considering attitudes toward Black migrants to Ireland.

The control sample was presented with the following list question:

The next questions are about your opinion on a few different issues in Ireland today. I am going to read out three things that

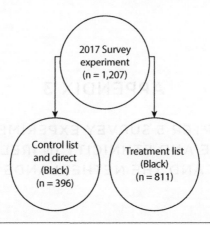

FIGURE AP.3 Design of the chapter 5 survey experiment conducted in Ireland

you may or may not support. After I read all three, just tell me HOW MANY of them you support. I don't want to know which statements, just HOW MANY.

(1) Higher weekly state pension
(2) Lower tax on diesel
(3) Bigger fines for litter

After the list question, the control sample was given the following direct question:

Would you support more Black people coming to live in Ireland?

The treatment sample was given the same list question but with four items listed instead of three. The additional focal item was worded as follows:

(4) More Black people coming to live in Ireland

The survey experiment conducted in the Netherlands considered the intersection of race and migration using the racial composition of the country as a reference. This approach was similar to that used by the European Social Survey to measure overt attitudes. The experiment was added to the Longitudinal Internet Studies for the Social Sciences (LISS) panel,[4] which was part of the Measurement and Experimentation in the Social Sciences project. Data were collected through an online survey. The sample was a true probability sample, and the original data are available at the LISS panel data archive.[5] The experiment was conducted in 2014, and some results were published via peer review in 2019.[6] All study collaborators are mentioned in chapter 5.

Figure ap.4 shows the design of the list experiment conducted in the Netherlands. The design of the experiment targeted the intersection of race and migration by considering attitudes toward migrants of the same or a different race or ethnicity from that of most of the Dutch population. Each of the three experimental groups that received a control list were random subsamples of the overall sample. All survey content was presented in Dutch. (Of note, there was an additional control list group that did not have a direct question relevant to this analysis; that question will be discussed in appendix 4.)

The control sample was presented with the following list question:

Of the following three statements, HOW MANY of them do you AGREE with? We don't want to know which statements, just HOW MANY.

(1)   The Netherlands should increase assistance to the poor.
(2)   The Netherlands should decrease the tax on petrol and diesel.
(3)   The Netherlands should allow large corporations to pollute the environment.

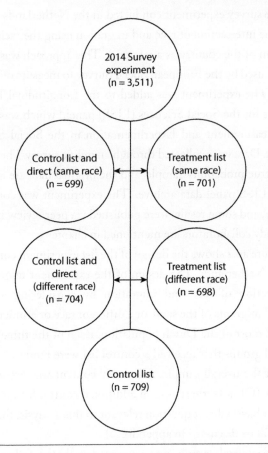

FIGURE AP.4 Design of the chapter 5 survey experiment conducted in the Netherlands

Two independent control samples were given one of the following direct questions:

Do you think the Netherlands should allow people of the same race or ethnic group as most Dutch people to come and live here?

Do you think the Netherlands should allow people of a different race or ethnic group from most Dutch people to come and live here?

Two treatment samples were given the same list question but with four items listed instead of three. The additional focal item was worded in one of the following ways:

(4) The Netherlands should allow people of the same race or ethnic group as most Dutch people to come and live here.

(4) The Netherlands should allow people of a different race or ethnic group from most Dutch people to come and live here.

As with the experiments described in other chapters, the design used in Ireland and the Netherlands permitted the direct comparison of covert and overt responses. The results showed the prevalence of agreement with the focal items and the difference between this covert estimate and that derived from direct interaction, which provided insight into the extent to which certain attitudes were strategically masked.

APPENDIX 4

CHAPTER 6 SURVEY EXPERIMENTS: MUSLIM MIGRANTS IN THE UNITED STATES, IRELAND, AND THE NETHERLANDS

Chapter 6 considered three list experiments conducted in the United States, Ireland, and the Netherlands. In the United States, similar to the design of the survey experiment described in chapter 3, the experiment was fielded using an online survey. The results from the U.S. study were published via peer review in 2015.[1] As mentioned in appendix 1, this survey experiment was part of a project developed to facilitate access to representative panels and implement experimental designs in the United States called Time-Sharing Experiments for the Social Sciences, funded by the National Science Foundation. The data for this study are publicly available.[2]

Figure ap.5 shows the design of the list experiment used in the United States. The study compared attitudes toward Muslim and Christian legal migrants to the United States.

The control sample was presented with the following list question:

Below you will read three things that sometimes people oppose or are against. After you read all three, just tell us HOW MANY of them you OPPOSE. We do not want to know which ones, just HOW MANY.

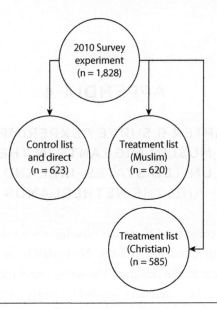

FIGURE AP.5 Design of the chapter 6 survey experiment conducted in the United States

(1) The federal government increasing assistance to the poor
(2) Professional athletes making millions of dollars per year
(3) Large corporations polluting the environment

After the list question, participants in the control sample were given one of the following direct questions:

Do you support or oppose granting citizenship to a legal immigrant who was Muslim?

Do you support or oppose granting citizenship to a legal immigrant who was Christian?

The treatment sample was given the same list question but with four items listed instead of three. The additional focal item was worded in one of the following ways:

(4) Granting citizenship to a legal immigrant who was Muslim

(4) Granting citizenship to a legal immigrant who was Christian

In Ireland, similar to the experiment described in chapter 5, the data were collected from the Economic Sentiment Monitor (ESM), which involved repeated cross-sectional data collection carried out by the Economic and Social Research Institute in Dublin.[3] As mentioned in appendix 3, the ESM was a telephone survey that used post-stratification, within-household weights derived from the Irish Labour Force Survey[4] to guarantee a representative sample of the Irish population. The experiment was fielded in 2019, and results were published in 2020 and 2022.[5] All study collaborators are mentioned in chapter 6.

Figure ap. 6 shows the design of the list experiment conducted in Ireland. The study targeted the intersection of religion and migration by considering attitudes toward Muslim migrants to Ireland.

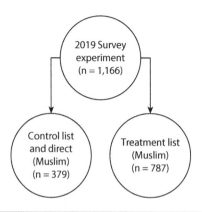

FIGURE AP.6 Design of the chapter 6 survey experiment conducted in Ireland

The control sample was presented with the following list question:

> The next questions are about your opinion on a few different issues in Ireland today. I am going to read out three things that you may or may not support. After I read all three, just tell me HOW MANY of them you support. I don't want to know which statements, just HOW MANY.
>
> (1)   Higher weekly state pension
> (2)   Lower tax on diesel
> (3)   Bigger fines for litter

After the list question, the control sample was given the following direct question:

> Would you support more Muslim people coming to live in Ireland?

The treatment sample was given the same list question but with four items listed instead of three. The additional focal item was worded as follows:

> (4)   More Muslim people coming to live in Ireland

The interpretation of the results was intuitive, with the difference between the mean response to the control list and the mean response to the treatment list identifying the proportion of the sample that supported Muslim migration to Ireland. Because individual responses were unknown, they provided an indication of covert sentiment. The sample that received the control list also received the direct question, which measured overt support for the migration of Muslims to Ireland. The difference between the overt and covert responses shows the percentage of the sample who indicated support only when anonymity was provided, which was the proportion who masked antipathy in the absence of anonymity.

As with the survey experiment described in chapter 5, the experiment conducted in the Netherlands was added to the Longitudinal Internet Studies for the Social Sciences (LISS) panel,[6] which was part of the Measurement and Experimentation in the Social Sciences project. Data were collected via an online survey. The sample was a true probability sample, and the original data are available at the LISS panel data archive.[7] The experiment was conducted in 2014, and some results were published in 2020.[8] All study collaborators are mentioned in chapter 6.

Figure ap. 7 shows the design of the list experiment conducted in the Netherlands. The study targeted attitudes toward Muslim newcomers and offers insight into the overlapping frames of religion and migrant status. All survey content was presented in Dutch. (Of note, the control list group was the same as that described in appendix 3. This group was a random subsample of the overall sample and independent of the group given the direct question.)

The control sample was presented with the following list question:

Of the following three statements, HOW MANY of them do you AGREE with? We don't want to know which statements, just HOW MANY.

(1) The Netherlands should increase assistance to the poor.
(2) The Netherlands should decrease the tax on petrol and diesel.
(3) The Netherlands should allow large corporations to pollute the environment.

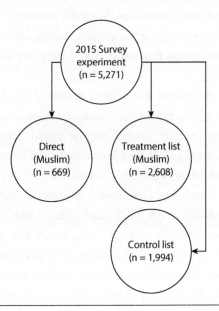

FIGURE AP.7 Design of the chapter 6 survey experiment conducted in the Netherlands

An independent control sample was also given the following direct question:

Do you think the Netherlands should allow Muslim people to come and live here?

Two treatment samples were given the same list question but with four items listed instead of three. The additional focal item was worded in one of the following ways:

(4) The Netherlands should allow Muslim people to come and live here.

(4) The Netherlands should allow people of a different race or ethnic group from most Dutch people to come and live here.

As with the experiments described in other chapters, the design used in Ireland and the Netherlands permitted the direct comparison of covert and overt responses. The results showed the prevalence of agreement with the focal items and the difference between this covert estimate and that derived from direct interaction, which provided insight into the extent to which certain attitudes were strategically masked.

APPENDIX 5

CHAPTER 7 SURVEY EXPERIMENT: PEOPLE, IMMIGRANTS, AND REFUGEES IN NORWAY

The survey experiment described in chapter 7 was embedded in the seventh wave of the Norwegian Citizen Panel,[1] a representative panel survey of the Norwegian population jointly administered at the time by the Faculty of Social Sciences at the University of Bergen and the Uni Research Rokkan Centre. The recruitment of panel members and the data collection were completed in partnership with the private data collection company ideas2evidence based on a sample drawn from Norway's National Registry, available from the Norwegian Tax Administration. Data were collected via an online survey, and the sample was representative of the adult population of Norway aged eighteen years and older. Participants were recruited via email, postal mail, and text message (which would be followed by a telephone call if a number was ascertainable). The experiment was conducted in 2016, and some results were published in 2020.[2] All collaborators are mentioned in chapter 7.

Figure ap.8 shows the design of the list experiment conducted in Norway. The study targeted attitudes toward Muslim newcomers and offers insight into the overlapping frames of refugee status and religion. All survey content was presented in Norwegian. (Of note, the Norwegian Citizen Panel included independent subsamples of the initial sample for all list and direct questions.)

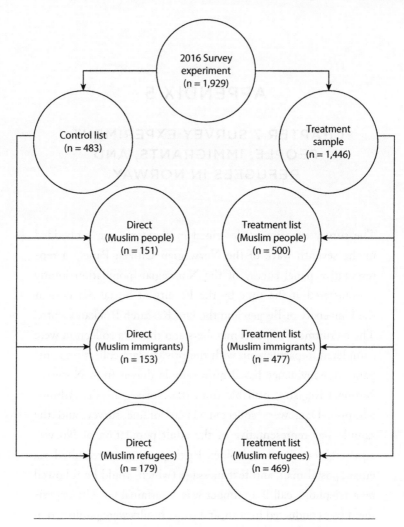

FIGURE AP.8 Design of the chapter 7 survey experiment conducted in Norway

An independent control sample was presented with the following list question:

> Of the following three statements, HOW MANY of them do you AGREE with? We don't want to know which statements, just HOW MANY.

(1) Norway should increase assistance to the poor.
(2) Norway should decrease the tax on petrol and diesel.
(3) Norway should allow large corporations to pollute the environment.

Three independent control samples were given the same list question and then one of the following direct questions:

> Should Norway allow people from Muslim countries to come and live here?
>
> Should Norway allow immigrants from Muslim countries to come and live here?
>
> Should Norway allow refugees from Muslim countries to come and live here?

Three treatment samples were given the same list question but with four items listed instead of three. The additional focal item was worded in one of the following ways:

(4) Norway should allow people from Muslim countries to come and live here.
(4) Norway should allow immigrants from Muslim countries to come and live here.
(4) Norway should allow refugees from Muslim countries to come and live here.

Subtracting the mean response to the control list from the mean response to the treatment list provided the covert measure of the proportion who agreed with the relevant focal item (e.g., the proportion who agreed that Norway should allow refugees from Muslim countries). The direct question measured overt support for the same questions, and the difference between the overt and covert responses shows the percentage of the sample who indicated support only when absolute and permanent anonymity was provided.

NOTES

INTRODUCTION

1. Oksana Yakushko, *Modern-Day Xenophobia: Critical Historical and The-oretical Perspectives on the Roots of Anti-immigrant Prejudice* (New York: Springer, 2018).
2. Tabish Khair, *The New Xenophobia* (Oxford: Oxford University Press, 2016).
3. James Dennison and Andrew Geddes, "A Rising Tide? The Salience of Immigration and the Rise of Anti-immigration Political Parties in Western Europe," *Political Quarterly* 90, no. 1 (2019): 107–16.
4. Daniel Stockemer, "The Economic Crisis (2009–2013) and Electoral Support for the Radical Right in Western Europe—Some New and Unexpected Findings," *Social Science Quarterly* 98, no. 5 (2017): 1536–53.
5. Alin M. Ceobanu and Xavier Escandell, "Comparative Analyses of Public Attitudes Toward Immigrants and Immigration Using Multi-national Survey Data: A Review of Theories and Research," *Annual Review of Sociology* 36 (2010): 309–28; Jens Hainmueller and Daniel J. Hopkins, "Public Attitudes Toward Immigration," *Annual Review of Political Science* 17 (2014): 225–49.
6. Mathew J. Creighton, Amaney Jamal, and Natalia C. Malancu, "Has Opposition to Immigration Increased in the United States After the Economic Crisis? An Experimental Approach," *International Migration Review* 49, no. 3 (2015): 727–56; Mathew J. Creighton and Amaney Jamal, "Does Islam Play a Role in Anti-immigrant Sentiment? An Experimental

Approach," *Social Science Research* 53 (2015): 89–103; Mathew J. Creighton and Amaney A. Jamal, "An Overstated Welcome: Brexit and Intentionally Masked Anti-immigrant Sentiment in the UK," *Journal of Ethnic and Migration Studies* 48, no. 5 (2022): 1051–71; Frances McGinnity, Mathew Creighton, and Éamonn Fahey, *Hidden Versus Revealed Attitudes: A List Experiment on Support for Minorities in Ireland* (Dublin: Economic and Social Research Institute, Irish Human Rights and Equality Commission, 2020); Mathew J. Creighton, Peter Schmidt, and Diana Zavala-Rojas, "Race, Wealth and the Masking of Opposition to Immigrants in the Netherlands," *International Migration* 57, no. 1 (2019): 245–63; Mathew J. Creighton and Zan Strabac, "Party Affiliation and Support for Muslim Newcomers: Masked Opposition in the Norwegian Context," *European Societies* 22, no. 4 (2020): 480–502.

7. Hart Blanton and James Jaccard, "Unconscious Racism: A Concept in Pursuit of a Measure," *Annual Review of Sociology* 34 (2008): 277–97.

8. Eduardo Bonilla-Silva, *Racism Without Racists: Color-Blind Racism and the Persistence of Racial Inequality in the United States* (Lanham, MD: Rowman & Littlefield, 2006); Meghan A. Burke, "Colorblind Racism: Identities, Ideologies, and Shifting Subjectivities," *Sociological Perspectives* 60, no. 5 (2017): 857–65.

9. Blanton and Jaccard, "Unconscious Racism"; Bonilla-Silva, *Racism Without Racists*; Eduardo Bonilla-Silva, "The Structure of Racism in Color-Blind, 'Post-racial' America," *American Behavioral Scientist* 59, no. 11 (2015): 1358–76; Douglas Hartmann et al., "Colorblindness as Identity: Key Determinants, Relations to Ideology, and Implications for Attitudes About Race and Policy," *Sociological Perspectives* 60, no. 5 (2017): 866–88.

10. Anthony G. Greenwald, Debbie E. McGhee, and Jordan L. K. Schwartz, "Measuring Individual Differences in Implicit Cognition: The Implicit Association Test," *Journal of Personality and Social Psychology* 74, no. 6 (1998): 1464; Frederick L. Oswald et al., "Predicting Ethnic and Racial Discrimination: A Meta-analysis of IAT Criterion Studies," *Journal of Personality and Social Psychology* 105, no. 2 (2013): 171; Anthony G. Greenwald, Mahzarin R. Banaji, and Brian A. Nosek, "Statistically Small Effects of the Implicit Association Test Can Have Societally Large Effects," *Journal of Personality and Social Psychology* 108, no. 4 (2015): 553.

11. Robert K. Merton, *Social Theory and Social Structure* (New York: Simon & Schuster, 1968).

12. Creighton and Jamal, "Does Islam Play a Role"; Creighton and Jamal, "An Overstated Welcome."

13. George Herbert Mead, *Mind, Self and Society*, ed. Charles W. Morris (Chicago: University of Chicago Press, 1934).

14. Herbert Blumer, "Race Prejudice as a Sense of Group Position," *Pacific Sociological Review* 1, no. 1 (1958): 3–7; Lawrence Bobo and Vincent L. Hutchings, "Perceptions of Racial Group Competition: Extending Blumer's Theory of Group Position to a Multiracial Social Context," *American Sociological Review* (1996): 951–72.

15. Erving Goffman, *Stigma: Notes on the Management of Spoiled Identity* (New York: Simon & Schuster, 1963).

16. Cas Mudde, *Populist Radical Right Parties in Europe* (Cambridge: Cambridge University Press, 2007).

17. Leonce Röth, Alexandre Afonso, and Dennis C. Spies, "The Impact of Populist Radical Right Parties on Socio-economic Policies," *European Political Science Review* 10, no. 3 (2018): 325–50; Jasper Muis and Tim Immerzeel, "Causes and Consequences of the Rise of Populist Radical Right Parties and Movements in Europe," *Current Sociology* 65, no. 6 (2017): 909–30; Matt Golder, "Far Right Parties in Europe," *Annual Review of Political Science* 19 (2016): 477–97; Thomas Greven, *The Rise of Right-Wing Populism in Europe and the United States: A Comparative Perspective* (Washington, DC: Friedrich Ebert Foundation, 2016), 1–8; Cas Mudde, "Three Decades of Populist Radical Right Parties in Western Europe: So What?," *European Journal of Political Research* 52, no. 1 (2013): 1–19.

18. Wouter Van der Brug, Meindert Fennema, and Jean Tillie, "Anti-immigrant Parties in Europe: Ideological or Protest Vote?," *European Journal of Political Research* 37, no. 1 (2000): 77–102; Kai Arzheimer, "Contextual Factors and the Extreme Right Vote in Western Europe, 1980–2002," *American Journal of Political Science* 53, no. 2 (2009): 259–75; Paul Hainsworth, *The Extreme Right in Europe* (London: Routledge, 2008); Swen Hutter and Hanspeter Kriesi, "Movements of the Left, Movements of the Right Reconsidered," in *Future of Social Movement Research: Dynamics, Mechanisms, and Processes*, ed. Jacquelien van Stekelenburg,

Conny Roggeband, and Bert Klandermans (Minneapolis: University of Minnesota Press, 2013): 281–98.

19. John B. Taylor, *The Financial Crisis and the Policy Responses: An Empirical Analysis of What Went Wrong*, Working Paper 14631 (Cambridge, MA: National Bureau of Economic Research, 2009).

20. Creighton and Jamal, "An Overstated Welcome."

21. Bonilla-Silva, "The Structure of Racism."

22. Narzanin Massoumi, David Miller, and Tom Mills, "Islamophobia, Social Movements and the State: For a Movement-Centered Approach," in *What Is Islamophobia? Racism, Social Movements and the State*, ed. Narzanin Massoumi, Tom Mills, and David Miller (London: Pluto, 2017), 3–32.

1. WHO IS THE XENOPHOBE?

1. Georg Simmel, "The Stranger," in *Georg Simmel on Individuality and Social Forms*, ed. Donald N. Levine (Chicago: University of Chicago Press, 1971).

2. E.g., Shaun Best, *The Stranger* (London: Routledge, 2019).

3. Edward Said, *Orientalism* (New York: Pantheon, 1978).

4. Nasar Meer, "Racialization and Religion: Race, Culture and Difference in the Study of Antisemitism and Islamophobia," *Ethnic and Racial Studies* 36, no. 3 (2013): 385–98.

5. Narzanin Massoumi, David Miller, and Tom Mills, "Islamophobia, Social Movements and the State: For a Movement-Centered Approach," in *What Is Islamophobia? Racism, Social Movements and the State*, ed. Narzanin Massoumi, Tom Mills, and David Miller (London: Pluto, 2017), 3–32.

6. Mathew J. Creighton and Amaney A. Jamal, "An Overstated Welcome: Brexit and Intentionally Masked Anti-immigrant Sentiment in the UK," *Journal of Ethnic and Migration Studies* 48, no. 5 (2022): 1051–71.

7. Mathew J. Creighton and Zan Strabac, "Party Affiliation and Support for Muslim Newcomers: Masked Opposition in the Norwegian Context," *European Societies* 22, no. 4 (2020): 480–502.

8. Creighton and Strabac, "Party Affiliation."

9. Mathew J. Creighton and Amaney Jamal, "Does Islam Play a Role in Anti-immigrant Sentiment? An Experimental Approach," *Social Science Research* 53 (2015): 89–103.

10. Creighton and Jamal, "An Overstated Welcome."

11. Wojciech Adamek and Janusz Radwan-Pragłowski, "Ludwik Gumplo-wicz: A Forgotten Classic of European Sociology," *Journal of Classical Sociology* 6, no. 3 (2006): 381–98.

12. Thomas J. Curran, "Assimilation and Nativism," *International Migration Digest* 3, no. 1 (1966): 15–25.

13. Alina Rzepnikowska, "Racism and Xenophobia Experienced by Polish Migrants in the UK Before and After Brexit Vote," *Journal of Ethnic and Migration Studies* 45, no. 1 (2019): 61–77.

14. Jens Hainmueller, Michael J. Hiscox, and Yotam Margalit, "Do Concerns About Labor Market Competition Shape Attitudes Toward Immigration? New Evidence," *Journal of International Economics* 97, no. 1 (2015): 193–207.

15. Sergi Pardos-Prado and Carla Xena, "Skill Specificity and Attitudes Toward Migration," *American Journal of Political Science* 63, no. 2 (2019): 286–304.

16. Creighton and Jamal, "An Overstated Welcome"; Creighton and Jamal, "Does Islam Play a Role."

17. Mathew J. Creighton, Peter Schmidt, and Diana Zavala-Rojas, "Race, Wealth and the Masking of Opposition to Immigrants in the Netherlands," *International Migration* 57, no. 1 (2019): 245–63.

18. Creighton and Jamal, "An Overstated Welcome."

19. David Pegg and Rob Evans, "Racist Royals? Buckingham Palace Banned Ethnic Minorities from Office Roles," *Irish Times*, June 3, 2021, https://www.irishtimes.com/life-and-style/people/racist-royals-buckingham-palace-banned-ethnic-minorities-from-office-roles-1.4583090.

20. Richard Rothstein, *The Color of Law: A Forgotten History of How Our Government Segregated America* (New York: Liveright, 2017).

21. Eduardo Bonilla-Silva, *Racism Without Racists: Color-Blind Racism and the Persistence of Racial Inequality in the United States* (Lanham, MD: Rowman & Littlefield, 2006); Eduardo Bonilla-Silva, "The Structure of Racism in Color-Blind, 'Post-racial' America," *American Behavioral Scientist* 59, no. 11 (2015): 1358–76.

22. Chloë FitzGerald et al., "Interventions Designed to Reduce Implicit Prejudices and Implicit Stereotypes in Real World Contexts: a Systematic Review," *BMC Psychology* 7, no. 1 (2019): 1–12.

2. THE STIGMA OF INTOLERANCE

1. Erving Goffman, *Stigma: Notes on the Management of Spoiled Identity* (New York: Simon & Schuster, 1963).

2. Goffman, *Stigma*, 4.

3. Erving Goffman, *The Presentation of Self in Everyday Life* (London: Allen Lane, 1959), 35.

4. Goffman, *Stigma*, 73.

5. Mathew J. Creighton and Amaney Jamal, "Does Islam Play a Role in Anti-immigrant Sentiment? An Experimental Approach," *Social Science Research* 53 (2015): 89–103.

6. Herbert Blumer, *Society as Symbolic Interaction* (Berkeley: University of California Press, 1969).

7. Herbert Blumer, "Public Opinion and Public Opinion Polling," *American Sociological Review* 13 (1948): 547.

8. David M. Douglas, "Doxing: A Conceptual Analysis," *Ethics and Information Technology* 18, no. 3 (2016): 199–210.

9. Ivar Krumpal, "Determinants of Social Desirability Bias in Sensitive Surveys: A Literature Review," *Quality & Quantity* 47, no. 4 (2013): 2025–47;; Roger Tourangeau and Ting Yan, "Sensitive Questions in Surveys," *Psychological Bulletin* 133, no. 5 (2007): 859.

10. Mathew J. Creighton, Peter Schmidt, and Diana Zavala-Rojas, "Race, Wealth and the Masking of Opposition to Immigrants in the Netherlands," *International Migration* 57, no. 1 (2019): 245–63; Mathew J. Creighton et al., "Application of a List Experiment at the Population Level: The Case of Opposition to Immigration in the Netherlands," in *Experimental Methods in Survey Research: Techniques That Combine Random Sampling with Random Assignment*, ed. Paul Lavrakas et al. (Hoboken, NJ: John Wiley, 2019), 181–93.

11. Saris and Gallhofer, *Design, Evaluation, and Analysis.*

12. Derek L. Phillips and Kevin J. Clancy, "Some Effects of 'Social Desirability' in Survey Studies," *American Journal of Sociology* 77, no. 5 (1972): 921–40.

13. Creighton, Schmidt, and Zavala-Rojas, "Race, Wealth."

14. Benjamin R. Knoll, "Implicit Nativist Attitudes, Social Desirability, and Immigration Policy Preferences," *International Migration Review* 47, no. 1 (2013): 132–65.

15. Benjamin R. Knoll, "Assessing the Effect of Social Desirability on Nativism Attitude Responses," *Social Science Research* 42, no. 6 (2013): 1587–98.

16. Alexander L. Janus, "The Influence of Social Desirability Pressures on Expressed Immigration Attitudes," *Social Science Quarterly* 91, no. 4 (2010): 928–46; Mathew J. Creighton, Amaney Jamal, and Natalia C. Malancu, "Has Opposition to Immigration Increased in the United States After the Economic Crisis? An Experimental Approach," *International Migration Review* 49, no. 3 (2015): 727–56.

17. Galit Gordoni and Peter Schmidt, "The Decision to Participate in Social Surveys: The Case of the Arab Minority in Israel—An Application of the Theory of Reasoned Action," *International Journal of Public Opinion Research* 22, no. 3 (2010): 364–91.

18. Philip M. Podsakoff et al., "Common Method Biases in Behavioral Research: A Critical Review of the Literature and Recommended Remedies," *Journal of Applied Psychology* 88, no. 5 (2003): 879–903.

19. Anthony G. Greenwald, Debbie E. McGhee, and Jordan L. K. Schwartz, "Measuring Individual Differences in Implicit Cognition: The Implicit Association Test," *Journal of Personality and Social Psychology* 74, no. 6 (1998): 1464; Anthony G. Greenwald, Mahzarin R. Banaji, and Brian A. Nosek, "Statistically Small Effects of the Implicit Association Test Can Have Societally Large Effects," *Journal of Personality and Social Psychology* 108, no. 4 (2015): 553.

20. Neil Malhotra, Yotam Margalit, and Cecilia Hyunjung Mo, "Economic Explanations for Opposition to Immigration: Distinguishing Between Prevalence and Conditional Impact," *American Journal of Political Science* 57, no. 2 (2013): 391–410.

21. Mathew J. Creighton, Éamonn Fahey, and Frances McGinnity, "Immigration, Identity, and Anonymity: Intentionally Masked Intolerance in Ireland," *International Migration Review* 56, no. 3 (2022): 881–910.

22. Graeme Blair and Kosuke Imai, "Statistical Analysis of List Experiments," *Political Analysis* 20, no. 1 (2012): 47–77.

23. Greenwald, McGhee, and Schwartz, "Measuring Individual Differences."

24. Frederick L. Oswald et al., "Predicting Ethnic and Racial Discrimination: A Meta-analysis of IAT Criterion Studies," *Journal of Personality and Social Psychology* 105, no. 2 (2013): 171.

25. Greenwald, Banaji, and Nosek, "Statistically Small Effects."

3. IF THERE ARE NO DOGS, WHY WHISTLE? INTOLERANCE AND THE XENOPHOBIC SEEDS OF POPULISM

1. Alin M. Ceobanu and Xavier Escandell, "Comparative Analyses of Public Attitudes Toward Immigrants and Immigration Using Multinational Survey Data: A Review of Theories and Research," *Annual Review of Sociology* 36 (2010): 317.

2. Pyong Gap Min, "A Comparison of the Korean Minorities in China and Japan," *International Migration Review* 26, no. 1 (1992): 4–21.

3. "UCD by Numbers," University College Dublin, https://www.ucd.ie /about-ucd/about/ucdbynumbers/. Accessed June 21, 2023.

4. Jens Hainmueller and Daniel J. Hopkins, "Public Attitudes Toward Immigration," *Annual Review of Political Science* 17 (2014): 225–49.

5. Rafaela M. Dancygier and Michael J. Donnelly, "Sectoral Economies, Economic Contexts, and Attitudes Toward Immigration," *Journal of Politics* 75, no. 1 (2013): 17–35.

6. Kenneth F. Scheve and Matthew J. Slaughter, "Labor Market Competition and Individual Preferences Over Immigration Policy," *Review of Economics and Statistics* 83, no. 1 (2001): 133–45; Anna Maria Mayda, "Who Is Against Immigration? A Cross-Country Investigation of Individual Attitudes Toward Immigrants," *Review of Economics and Statistics* 88, no. 3 (2006): 510–30; Lauren McLaren and Mark Johnson, "Resources, Group Conflict and Symbols: Explaining Anti-immigration Hostility in Britain," *Political Studies* 55, no. 4 (2007): 709–32.

7. George J. Borjas, Richard B. Freeman, and Lawrence F. Katz, "Searching for the Effect of Immigration on the Labor Market," *American Economic Review* 86, no. 2 (1996): 246–51.

8. Muzafer Sherif, *In Common Predicament: Social Psychology of Intergroup Conflict and Cooperation* (Boston, MA; Houghton Mifflin, 1970).

9. Jens Hainmueller and Michael J. Hiscox, "Attitudes Toward Highly Skilled and Low-Skilled Immigration: Evidence from a Survey Experiment," *American Political Science Review* 104, no. 1 (2010): 61–84.

10. Jens Hainmueller and Michael J. Hiscox, "Educated Preferences: Explaining Attitudes Toward Immigration in Europe," *International Organization* 61, no. 2 (2007): 399–442.

11. Hainmueller and Hiscox, "Attitudes Toward Highly Skilled and Low-Skilled Immigration"; Jens Hainmueller, Michael J. Hiscox, and Yotam

Margalit, "Do Concerns About Labor Market Competition Shape Attitudes Toward Immigration? New Evidence," *Journal of International Economics* 97, no. 1 (2015): 193–207.

12. Mayda, "Who Is Against Immigration?"

13. Scheve and Slaughter, "Labor Market Competition."

14. Thomas J. Espenshade and Katherine Hempstead, "Contemporary American Attitudes Toward US Immigration," *International Migration Review* 30, no. 2 (1996): 535–70; Lauren M. McLaren, "Anti-immigrant Prejudice in Europe: Contact, Threat Perception, and Preferences for the Exclusion of Migrants," *Social Forces* 81, no. 3 (2003): 909–36; Christian Dustmann and Ian P. Preston, "Racial and Economic Factors in Attitudes to Immigration," *B. E. Journal of Economic Analysis & Policy* 7, no. 1 (2007); John Sides and Jack Citrin, "European Opinion About Immigration: The Role of Identities, Interests and Information," *British Journal of Political Science* 37, no. 3 (2007): 477–504.

15. Charles R. Chandler and Yung-mei Tsai, "Social Factors Influencing Immigration Attitudes: An Analysis of Data from the General Social Survey," *Social Science Journal* 38, no. 2 (2001): 177–88; Ted Brader, Nicholas A. Valentino, and Elizabeth Suhay, "What Triggers Public Opposition to Immigration? Anxiety, Group Cues, and Immigration Threat," *American Journal of Political Science* 52, no. 4 (2008): 959–78.

16. Hainmueller and Hiscox, "Attitudes Toward Highly Skilled and Low-Skilled Immigration."

17. Hainmueller and Hopkins, "Public Attitudes Toward Immigration."

18. Bart Meuleman, "Perceived Economic Threat and Anti-immigration Attitudes: Effects of Immigrant Group Size and Economic Conditions Revisited," in *Cross-Cultural Analysis: Methods and Applications*, ed. Eldad Davidov, Peter Schmidt, and Jaak Billiet (New York: Routledge: 2011), 281–310.

19. John Komlos, *The Economic Roots of the Rise of Trumpism*, CESifo Working Paper Series No. 6868 (Munich: Munich Society for the Promotion of Economic Research, 2018), https://ssrn.com/abstract=3144271.

20. John B. Taylor, *The Financial Crisis and the Policy Responses: An Empirical Analysis of What Went Wrong*, Working Paper No. 14631 (Cambridge, MA: National Bureau of Economic Research, 2009).

21. Katharine M. Donato and Catalina Amuedo-Dorantes, "The Legal Landscape of US Immigration: An Introduction," *Russell Sage Foundation Journal of the Social Sciences* 6, no. 3 (2020): 1–16.

22. Cameron Ballard-Rosa, Amalie Jensen, and Kenneth Scheve, "Economic Decline, Social Identity, and Authoritarian Values in the United States," *International Studies Quarterly* 66, no. 1 (2022): sqab027.

23. Michael McQuarrie, "The Revolt of the Rust Belt: Place and Politics in the Age of Anger," *British Journal of Sociology* 68 (2017): S120–52.

24. Mathew J. Creighton, Amaney Jamal, and Natalia C. Malancu, "Has Opposition to Immigration Increased in the United States After the Economic Crisis? An Experimental Approach," *International Migration Review* 49, no. 3 (2015): 727–56.

25. See Creighton, Jamal, and Malancu, "Has Opposition to Immigration Increased," for a detailed description of the approach, sample, and results of the list experiment described in table 3.1.

26. Christopher P. Muste, "The Dynamics of Immigration Opinion in the United States, 1992–2012," *Public Opinion Quarterly* 77, no. 1 (2013): 398–416.

27. Significance is a contested idea in social science and statistics more broadly. I use it here to refer to values that, via some statistical test, can be shown to be different from zero. In this case, 95 percent of responses are expected to show a difference of more than zero. This cut point is admittedly arbitrary but does match widely used standards in the literature.

28. Creighton, Jamal, and Malancu, "Has Opposition to Immigration Increased."

29. Sabrina P. Ramet and Christine M. Hassenstab, "The Know Nothing Party: Three Theories About Its Rise and Demise," *Politics and Religion* 6, no. 3 (2013): 570–95.

30. Leonie Huddy and Alessandro Del Ponte, "The Rise of Populism in the USA: Nationalism, Race, and American Party Politics," in *The Psychology of Populism: The Tribal Challenge to Liberal Democracy*, ed. Joseph P. Forgas, William D. Crano, and Klaus Fiedler (New York: Routledge, 2021), 258–75.

4. REFERENDA AND BORDERS: BREXIT AND THE ROLE OF THE XENOPHOBE IN THE DIVISION OF EUROPE

1. Margit Fauser, Anne Friedrichs, and Levke Harders, "Migrations and Borders: Practices and Politics of Inclusion and Exclusion in Europe from the Nineteenth to the Twenty-First Century," *Journal of Borderlands Studies* 34, no. 4 (2019): 483–88.

2. For citizens of EU countries, the free movement of workers is a fundamental principle enshrined in Article 45 of the Treaty on the Functioning of the European Union and developed by EU secondary legislation
and the case law of the Court of Justice of the European Union. In
addition, some non-EU members of the European Economic Area
(i.e., Iceland, Liechtenstein, and Norway) are allowed similar rights.

3. European Commission, *Report from the Commission to the European
Parliament, the Council and the European Economic and Social Com-
mittee on the Implementation of Directive 2014/54/EU of the European
Parliament and of the Council of 16 April 2014 on Measures Facilitating
the Exercise of Rights Conferred on Workers in the Context of Freedom of
Movement for Workers* (Brussels: European Commission, 2018); Elena
Fries-Tersch, Matthew Jones, and Linus Siöland, *Annual Report on
Intra-EU Labour Mobility 2020* (Luxembourg: Publications Office of
the European Union, 2021).

4. Cas Mudde, *Populist Radical Right Parties in Europe* (Cambridge:
Cambridge University Press, 2007).

5. Timothy J. Hatton, "Public Opinion on Immigration in Europe: Preference and Salience," *European Journal of Political Economy* 66 (2021): 101969.

6. Gilles Ivaldi, "Contesting the EU in Times of Crisis: The Front National
and Politics of Euroscepticism in France," *Politics* 38, no. 3 (2018): 278–94.

7. Paul M. Sniderman and Louk Hagendoorn, *When Ways of Life Col-
lide: Multiculturalism and Its Discontents in the Netherlands* (Princeton,
NJ: Princeton University Press, 2007); Katharine Betts, *Ideology and
Immigration: Australia 1976 to 1987* (Melbourne: Melbourne University
Press, 1988); Thomas J. Espenshade and Katherine Hempstead, "Con-
temporary American Attitudes Toward US Immigration," *International
Migration Review* 30, no. 2 (1996): 535–70.

8. Sniderman and Hagendoorn, *When Ways of Life Collide*; Pierangelo
Isernia and Kaat Smets, "Revealing Preferences: Does Deliberation
Increase Ideological Awareness Among the Less Well Educated?,"
European Journal of Political Research 53, no. 3 (2014): 520–40.

9. Jasper Muis and Tim Immerzeel, "Causes and Consequences of the
Rise of Populist Radical Right Parties and Movements in Europe,"
Current Sociology 65, no. 6 (2017): 909–30; Matt Golder, "Far Right
Parties in Europe," *Annual Review of Political Science* 19 (2016): 477–97;
Thomas Greven, *The Rise of Right-Wing Populism in Europe and the*

United States: A Comparative Perspective (Washington, DC: Friedrich Ebert Foundation, 2016), 1–8; Cas Mudde, "Three Decades of Populist Radical Right Parties in Western Europe: So What?," *European Journal of Political Research* 52, no. 1 (2013): 1–19.

10. Leonce Röth, Alexandre Afonso, and Dennis C. Spies, "The Impact of Populist Radical Right Parties on Socio-economic Policies," *European Political Science Review* 10, no. 3 (2018): 325–50.

11. W. van de Brug, M. Fennema, and J. Tillie, "Why Some Anti-immigrant Parties Fail and Others Succeed: a Two-Step Model of Aggregate Electoral Support," *Comparative Political Studies* 38 (2005): 537–73; K. Arzheimer, "Contextual Factors and the Extreme Right Vote in Western Europe, 1980–2002," *American Journal of Political Science* 53 (2009): 259–75; P. Hainsworth, *Extreme Right in Western Europe* (New York: Routledge, 2008); S. Hutter, and H. Kriesi, "Movements of the Left, Movements of the Right Reconsidered," in *The Future of Social Movements Research*, ed. J. Van Stekelenburg, C. Roggeband and B. Klandermans (Minneapolis: University of Minnesota Press, 2013), 281–98.

12. Henning Finseraas, "Anti-immigration Attitudes, Support for Redistribution and Party Choice in Europe," in *Changing Social Equality: The Nordic Welfare Model in the 21st Century*, ed. Jon Kvist et al. (Bristol: Policy, 2012), 23–44.

13. Joost van Spanje, "The Wrong and the Right: A Comparative Analysis of 'Anti-immigration' and 'Far Right' Parties," *Government and Opposition* 46, no. 3 (2011): 293–320.

14. Mudde, "Three Decades."

15. The use of term *populist* is consistent with the literature but is captured mostly by political movements on the right. As such, it is a term of convenience, and historical examples of populism (e.g., Turkey, Argentina) suggest that a single definition of the term is not a reasonable goal. That said, rather than *right-wing populism* or *extreme right*, the general term *populism* will be used throughout.

16. Conor Gallagher, "Ireland First: Inside the Group Chat of Ireland's Latest Far-Right Political Party," *Irish Times* March 12, 2023, https://www.irishtimes.com/ireland/social-affairs/2023/03/12/ireland-first-becomes-a-political-party-but-will-anyone-vote-for-it/.

17. Xavier Medina Vidal, "Immigration Politics in the 2016 Election," *PS: Political Science & Politics* 51, no. 2 (2018): 304–308.

18. Robert Ford, Will Jennings, and Will Somerville, "Public Opinion, Responsiveness and Constraint: Britain's Three Immigration Policy Regimes," *Journal of Ethnic and Migration Studies* 41, no. 9 (2015): 1391–1411.

19. Ford, Jennings, and Somerville, "Public Opinion."

20. See the Vote Leave website: http://voteleavetakecontrol.org.

21. Technically, the designation of Vote Leave as the official pro-Brexit campaign entity by the UK Electoral Commission did not occur until April 13, 2016. That said, the writing was on the wall from an early stage.

22. Jenny Gross, "Britain's Gas Crisis, Explained," *New York Times*, September 28, 2021, https://www.nytimes.com/2021/09/28/world/europe/why-uk-fuel-shortage.html?smid=em-share.

23. Heather Stewart and Rowena Mason, "Nigel Farage's Anti-migrant Poster Reported to Police," *Guardian*, June 16, 2016, https://www.theguardian.com/politics/2016/jun/16/nigel-farage-defends-ukip-breaking-point-poster-queue-of-migrants#.

24. "The Brexit Result Had a Lasting Impact on Race and Religious Hate Crimes," Tell MAMA, October 13, 2016, https://tellmamauk.org/the-brexit-result-had-a-lasting-impact-on-race-and-religious-hate-crimes/; Hannah Corcoran and Kevin Smith, *Hate Crime, England and Wales, 2015/16*, Statistical Bulletin 11/16 (London: Home Office, 2016).

25. Joshua Matti and Yang Zhou, "The Political Economy of Brexit: Explaining the Vote," *Applied Economics Letters* 24, no. 16 (2017): 1131–34.

26. Mathew J. Creighton and Amaney A. Jamal, "An Overstated Welcome: Brexit and Intentionally Masked Anti-immigrant Sentiment in the UK," *Journal of Ethnic and Migration Studies* 48, no. 5 (2022): 1051–71.

27. Creighton and Jamal, "An Overstated Welcome."

28. Mathew J. Creighton and Amaney Jamal, "Does Islam Play a Role in Anti-immigrant Sentiment? An Experimental Approach," *Social Science Research* 53 (2015): 89–103.

5. COLOR-BLIND OR INTENTIONALLY LOOKING AWAY?

1. Eduardo Bonilla-Silva, *Racism Without Racists: Color-Blind Racism and the Persistence of Racial Inequality in America*, 5th ed. (Lanham, MD: Rowman & Littlefield, 2018).

2. Lincoln Quillian et al., "Meta-analysis of Field Experiments Shows No Change in Racial Discrimination in Hiring Over Time," *Proceedings of the National Academy of Sciences* 114, no. 41 (2017): 10870–75.

3. Hart Blanton and James Jaccard, "Unconscious Racism: A Concept in Pursuit of a Measure," *Annual Review of Sociology* 34 (2008): 277–97.

4. Bonilla-Silva, *Racism Without Racists*; Meghan A. Burke, "Colorblind Racism: Identities, Ideologies, and Shifting Subjectivities," *Sociological Perspectives* 60, no. 5 (2017): 857–65.

5. Blanton and Jaccard, "Unconscious Racism"; Bonilla-Silva, *Racism Without Racists*; Eduardo Bonilla-Silva, "The Structure of Racism in Color-Blind, 'Post-racial' America," *American Behavioral Scientist* 59, no. 11 (2015): 1358–76.

6. Mario L. Small and Devah Pager, "Sociological Perspectives on Racial Discrimination," *Journal of Economic Perspectives* 34, no. 2 (2020): 49–67.

7. Emily Blout and Patrick Burkart, "White Supremacist Terrorism in Charlottesville: Reconstructing 'Unite the Right,'" *Studies in Conflict & Terrorism* (2021): 1–22.

8. Fabian Virchow, "PEGIDA: Understanding the Emergence and Essence of Nativist Protest in Dresden," *Journal of Intercultural Studies* 37, no. 6 (2016): 541–55.

9. After winning twenty seats in the 2017 parliamentary elections, the PVV performed poorly in the 2019 provincial elections, losing twenty-six seats. This loss was not caused by a change in voting behavior; rather, it largely reflected a defection to an ideologically adjacent party, the Forum for Democracy (*Forum voor Democratie*).

10. Richard Wike, Bruce Stokes, and Katie Simmons, *Europeans Fear Wave of Refugees Will Mean More Terrorism, Fewer Jobs* (Washington, DC: Pew Research Center, 2016).

11. Toby Sterling and Anthony Deutsch, "Dutch Populist Wilders Acquitted of Inciting Discrimination," *Reuters*, September 4, 2020, https://www.reuters.com/article/uk-netherlands-wilders-idUKKBN25V1BQ.

12. Paul M. Sniderman and Louk Hagendoorn, *When Ways of Life Collide: Multiculturalism and Its Discontents in the Netherlands* (Princeton, NJ: Princeton University Press, 2007); Mathew J. Creighton, Peter Schmidt, and Diana Zavala-Rojas, "Race, Wealth and the Masking of Opposition to Immigrants in the Netherlands," *International Migration* 57, no. 1

(2019): 245–63; Mathew J. Creighton et al., "Application of a List Experiment at the Population Level: The Case of Opposition to Immigration in the Netherlands," in *Experimental Methods in Survey Research: Techniques That Combine Random Sampling with Random Assignment*, ed. Paul J. Lavrakas et al. (Hoboken, NJ: Wiley, 2019), 181–93.

13. Annette C. Scherpenzeel, "'True' Longitudinal and Probability-Based Internet Panels: Evidence From the Netherlands," in *Social and Behavioral Research and the Internet: Advances in Applied Methods and Research Strategies*, ed. Marcel Das, Peter Ester, and Lars Kaczmirek (New York: Routledge, 2018), 77–104.

14. Creighton et al., "Application of a List Experiment"; Creighton, Schmidt, and Zavala-Rojas, "Race, Wealth"; Mathew J. Creighton, "Stigma and the Meaning of Social Desirability: Concealed Islamophobia in the Netherlands," in *Understanding Survey Methodology: Sociological Theory and Applications*, ed. Philip S. Brenner (Cham: Springer, 2020), 115–42.

15. Kerby A. Miller, Bruce Boling, and David N. Doyle, "Emigrants and Exiles: Irish Cultures and Irish Emigration to North America, 1790–1922," *Irish Historical Studies* 22, no. 86 (1980): 97–125.

16. Kevin Kenny, "Race, Violence, and Anti-Irish Sentiment in the Nineteenth Century," in *Making the Irish American: History and Heritage of the Irish in the United States*, ed. J. J. Lee and Marion R. Casey (New York: New York University Press, 2006), 364–78.

17. Frances McGinnity et al., *Attitudes to Diversity in Ireland* (Dublin: Economic and Social Research Institute, Irish Human Rights and Equality Commission, 2018).

18. Thomas Turner and Christine Cross, "Do Attitudes to Immigrants Change in Hard Times? Ireland in a European Context," *European Societies* 17, no. 3 (2015): 372–95.

19. McGinnity et al., *Attitudes to Diversity in Ireland*.

20. Miller, Boling, and Doyle, "Emigrants and Exiles."

21. McGinnity et al., *Attitudes to Diversity in Ireland*.

22. Frances McGinnity, Mathew Creighton, and Éamonn Fahey, *Hidden Versus Revealed Attitudes: A List Experiment on Support for Minorities in Ireland* (Dublin: Economic and Social Research Institute, Irish Human Rights and Equality Commission, 2020); Mathew J. Creighton, Éamonn

Fahey, and Frances McGinnity, "Immigration, Identity, and Anonymity: Intentionally Masked Intolerance in Ireland," *International Migration Review* 56, no. 3 (2022): 881–910.

23. Mathew J. Creighton and Amaney Jamal, "Does Islam Play a Role in Anti-immigrant Sentiment? An Experimental Approach," *Social Science Research* 53 (2015): 89–103.

24. Christopher F. Karpowitz et al., "Experimenting with List Experiments: Interviewer Effects and Immigration Attitudes," *Public Opinion Quarterly* 87, no. 1 (2023): 69–91.

25. Abby Budiman et al., "Facts on U.S. Immigrants, 2018: Statistical Portrait of the Foreign-Born Population in the United States," Pew Research Center, August 20, 2020, https://www.pewresearch.org/hispanic/2020/08/20/facts-on-u-s-immigrants-previous-years-data/. Data are from the 1 percent samples of the 2010 and 2018 American Community Survey Integrated Public Use Microdata Series provided by the University of Minnesota.

26. Abby Budiman et al., "Facts on U.S. Immigrants, 2018."

27. Alessandra Bazo Vienrich and Mathew J. Creighton, "What's Left Unsaid? In-Group Solidarity and Ethnic and Racial Differences in Opposition to Immigration in the United States," *Journal of Ethnic and Migration Studies* 44, no. 13 (2018): 2240–55.

28. Bazo Vienrich and Creighton, "What's Left Unsaid?"

29. Bonilla-Silva, *Racism Without Racists.*

30. Jens Hainmueller, Michael J. Hiscox, and Yotam Margalit, "Do Concerns About Labor Market Competition Shape Attitudes Toward Immigration? New Evidence," *Journal of International Economics* 97, no. 1 (2015): 193–207.

31. Hainmueller, Hiscox, and Margalit, "Do Concerns About Labor Market Competition Shape Attitudes."

32. Philip Bump, "Donald Trump's Plan to Bar Muslim Immigrants from Entering the United States, Annotated," *Washington Post*, August 15, 2016, https://www.washingtonpost.com/news/the-fix/wp/2016/08/15/donald-trumps-plan-to-bar-immigrants-from-entering-the-united-states-annotated/.

33. Adam Liptak and Michael D. Shear,, "Trump's Travel Ban Is Upheld by Supreme Court," *New York Times*, June 26, 2018, https://www.nytimes.com/2018/06/26/us/politics/supreme-court-trump-travel

-ban.html#:~:text=WASHINGTON%20%E2%80%94%20The%20
Supreme%20Court%20upheld,migrants%20at%20the%20Mexican%20
border.

34. Natalie Alkiviadou, Jacob Mchangama, and Raghav Mendiratta, *Global Handbook on Hate Speech Laws* (Copenhagen: Justitia, 2020).

35. Blanton and Jaccard, "Unconscious Racism."

36. Behavioural Insights Team, *Unconscious Bias and Diversity Training— What the Evidence Says* (London: Behavioural Insights Team, 2020), https://assets.publishing.service.gov.uk/government/uploads/system /uploads/attachment_data/file/944431/20-12-14_UBT_BIT_report.pdf.

6. BEHIND A VEIL OF INTOLERANCE: ISLAMOPHOBIA AND OVERT XENOPHOBIC EXPRESSION

1. Ceri Peach and Günther Glebe, "Muslim Minorities in Western Europe," *Ethnic and Racial Studies* 18, no. 1 (1995): 26–45.

2. Michael Lipka, "Muslims and Islam: Key Findings in the U.S. and Around the World," Pew Research Center, August 9, 2017, https:// www.pewresearch.org/short-reads/2017/08/09/muslims-and-islam -key-findings-in-the-u-s-and-around-the-world/.

3. Drew DeSilver and David Masci, "World's Muslim Population More Widespread Than You Might Think," Pew Research Center, January 13, 2017, https://www.pewresearch.org/short-reads/2017/01/31/worlds -muslim-population-more-widespread-than-you-might-think/.

4. Besheer Mohamed, "New Estimates Show U.S. Muslim Population Continues to Grow," Pew Research Center, January 3, 2018, https:// www.pewresearch.org/short-reads/2018/01/03/new-estimates-show -u-s-muslim-population-continues-to-grow/.

5. Ferruh Yılmaz, "Right-Wing Hegemony and Immigration: How the Populist Far-Right Achieved Hegemony Through the Immigration Debate in Europe," *Current Sociology* 60, no. 3 (2012): 368–81.

6. Philip Bump, "Donald Trump's Plan to Bar Muslim Immigrants from Entering the United States, Annotated," *Washington Post*, August 15, 2016, https://www.washingtonpost.com/news/the-fix/wp/2016/08/15 /donald-trumps-plan-to-bar-immigrants-from-entering-the-united -states-annotated/.

7. DeSilver and Masci, "World's Muslim Population."
8. Mathew J. Creighton and Amaney Jamal, "Does Islam Play a Role in Anti-immigrant Sentiment? An Experimental Approach," *Social Science Research* 53 (2015): 89–103; Kerem Ozan Kalkan, Geoffrey C. Layman, and Eric M. Uslaner, " 'Bands of Others'? Attitudes Toward Muslims in Contemporary American Society," *Journal of Politics* 71, no. 3 (2009): 847–62; Amaney Jamal and Nadine Naber, eds., *Race and Arab Americans Before and After 9/11: From Invisible Citizens to Visible Subjects* (Syracuse, NY: Syracuse University Press, 2008).
9. Zan Strabac et al., "Wearing the Veil: Hijab, Islam and Job Qualifications as Determinants of Social Attitudes Towards Immigrant Women in Norway," *Ethnic and Racial Studies* 39, no. 15 (2016): 2665–82.
10. Zan Strabac and Ola Listhaug, "Anti-Muslim Prejudice in Europe: A Multilevel Analysis of Survey Data from 30 Countries," *Social Science Research* 37, no. 1 (2008): 268–86.
11. Marc Helbling, "Opposing Muslims and the Muslim Headscarf in Western Europe," *European Sociological Review* 30, no. 2 (2014): 242–57.
12. Strabac et al., "Wearing the Veil."
13. Costas Panagopoulos, "Trends: Arab and Muslim Americans and Islam in the Aftermath of 9/11," *Public Opinion Quarterly* 70, no. 4 (2006): 608–24; Victoria M. Esses, John F. Dovidio, and Gordon Hodson, "Public Attitudes Toward Immigration in the United States and Canada in Response to the September 11, 2001 'Attack on America,' " *Analyses of Social Issues and Public Policy* 2, no. 1 (2002): 69–85.
14. Jack G. Shaheen, "Reel Bad Arabs: How Hollywood Vilifies a People," *Annals of the American Academy of Political and Social Science* 588, no. 1 (2003): 171–93; Michael W. Suleiman, "Stereotypes, Public Opinion and Foreign Policy: The Impact on American-Arab Relations," *Journal of Arab Affairs* 1, no. 2 (1982): 147; Daniel Mandel, "Muslims on the Silver Screen," *Middle East Quarterly* 8 (2001): 19–30; Fawaz A. Gerges, "Islam and Muslims in the Mind of America," *Annals of the American Academy of Political and Social Science* 588, no. 1 (2003): 73–89.
15. Pew Research Center, *Muslim Americans: Middle Class and Mostly Mainstream* (Washington, DC: Pew Research Center, 2007), http://pewresearch.org/assets/pdf/muslim-americans.pdf.
16. Creighton and Jamal, "Does Islam Play a Role."

17. Daniel Boffey and Toby Helm, "Vote Leave Embroiled in Race Row Over Turkey Security Threat Claims," *Guardian*, May 22, 2016, https://www.theguardian.com/politics/2016/may/21/vote-leave-prejudice-turkey-eu-security-threat.

18. Giulia Evolvi, "Hate in a Tweet: Exploring Internet-Based Islamophobic Discourses," *Religions* 9, no. 10 (2018): 307.

19. Evolvi, "Hate in a Tweet."

20. Joshua Matti and Yang Zhou, "The Political Economy of Brexit: Explaining the Vote," *Applied Economics Letters* 24, no. 16 (2017): 1131–34.

21. Mathew J. Creighton and Amaney A. Jamal, "An Overstated Welcome: Brexit and Intentionally Masked Anti-immigrant Sentiment in the UK," *Journal of Ethnic and Migration Studies* 48, no. 5 (2022): 1051–71.

22. E. Daniel Kim, "Shamus Rahman Khan: Privilege: The Making of an Adolescent Elite at St. Paul's School," *Journal of Youth and Adolescence* 45 (2016): 239–41.

23. George J. Borjas, "The Economic Analysis of Immigration," in *Handbook of Labor Economics*, vol. 3A, ed. Orley C. Ashenfelter and David Card (Amsterdam: Elsevier Science, 1999), 1697–1760. Kenneth F. Scheve and Matthew J. Slaughter, "Labor Market Competition and Individual Preferences Over Immigration Policy," *Review of Economics and Statistics* 83, no. 1 (2001): 133–45; Anna Maria Mayda, "Who Is Against Immigration? A Cross-Country Investigation of Individual Attitudes Toward Immigrants," *Review of Economics and Statistics* 88, no. 3 (2006): 510–30; Gordon H. Hanson, Kenneth Scheve, and Matthew J. Slaughter, "Public Finance and Individual Preferences Over Globalization Strategies," *Economics & Politics* 19, no. 1 (2007): 1–33; Lauren McLaren and Mark Johnson, "Resources, Group Conflict and Symbols: Explaining Anti-immigration Hostility in Britain," *Political Studies* 55, no. 4 (2007): 709–32.

24. Jens Hainmueller and Daniel J. Hopkins, "Public Attitudes Toward Immigration," *Annual Review of Political Science* 17 (2014): 225–49; Alin M. Ceobanu and Xavier Escandell, "Comparative Analyses of Public Attitudes Toward Immigrants and Immigration Using Multinational Survey Data: A Review of Theories and Research," *Annual Review of Sociology* 36 (2010): 309–28; Silke L. Schneider, "Anti-immigrant Attitudes in Europe: Outgroup Size and Perceived Ethnic Threat," *European Sociological Review* 24, no. 1 (2008): 53–67.

242 • 6. BEHIND A VEIL OF INTOLERANCE

25. Jens Hainmueller and Michael J. Hiscox, "Educated Preferences: Explaining Attitudes Toward Immigration in Europe," *International Organization* 61, no. 2 (2007): 399–442.
26. Katerina Manevska and Peter Achterberg, "Immigration and Perceived Ethnic Threat: Cultural Capital and Economic Explanations," *European Sociological Review* 29, no. 3 (2013): 437–49.
27. Elisa Rustenbach, "Sources of Negative Attitudes Toward Immigrants in Europe: A Multi-level Analysis," *International Migration Review* 44, no. 1 (2010): 53–77.
28. Michael Savelkoul et al., "Anti-Muslim Attitudes in the Netherlands: Tests of Contradictory Hypotheses Derived from Ethnic Competition Theory and Intergroup Contact Theory," *European Sociological Review* 27, no. 6 (2011): 741–58.
29. Paul M. Sniderman and Louk Hagendoorn, *When Ways of Life Collide: Multiculturalism and Its Discontents in the Netherlands* (Princeton, NJ: Princeton University Press, 2007).
30. Richard Wike, Bruce Stokes, and Katie Simmons, *Europeans Fear Wave of Refugees Will Mean More Terrorism, Fewer Jobs* (Washington, DC: Pew Research Center, 2016).
31. Sniderman and Hagendoorn, *When Ways of Life Collide.*
32. Wike, Stokes, and Simmons, *Europeans Fear Wave of Refugees.*
33. "Census 2016 Profile 8 - Irish Travellers, Ethnicity and Religion," Central Statistics Office, accessed July 29, 2021, https://www.cso.ie/en/csolatestnews/presspages/2017/census2016profile8-irishtravellersethnicityandreligion/.
34. Éamonn Fahey, Frances McGinnity, and Raffaele Grotti, "Irish Attitudes to Muslim Immigrants," *Economic and Social Review* 50, no. 3 (2019): 491–514.
35. Bryan Fanning, *Migration and the Making of Ireland* (Bloomington: Indiana University Press, 2021).
36. Frances McGinnity, Mathew Creighton, and Éamonn Fahey, *Hidden Versus Revealed Attitudes: A List Experiment on Support for Minorities in Ireland* (Dublin: Economic and Social Research Institute, Irish Human Rights and Equality Commission, 2020); Mathew J. Creighton, Éamonn Fahey, and Frances McGinnity, "Immigration, Identity, and Anonymity: Intentionally Masked Intolerance in Ireland," *International Migration Review* 56, no. 3 (2022): 881–910.

37. Mathew J. Creighton et al., "Application of a List Experiment at the Population Level: The Case of Opposition to Immigration in the Netherlands," in *Experimental Methods in Survey Research: Techniques That Combine Random Sampling with Random Assignment*, ed. Paul J. Lavrakas et al. (Hoboken, NJ: Wiley, 2019), 181–93; Mathew J. Creighton, Peter Schmidt, and Diana Zavala-Rojas, "Race, Wealth and the Masking of Opposition to Immigrants in the Netherlands," *International Migration* 57, no. 1 (2019): 245–63; Mathew J. Creighton, "Stigma and the Meaning of Social Desirability: Concealed Islamophobia in the Netherlands," in *Understanding Survey Methodology: Sociological Theory and Applications*, ed. Philip S. Brenner (Cham: Springer, 2020), 115–42.
38. Drew DeSilver and David Masci, "World's Muslim Population More Widespread Than You Might Think," Pew Research Center, January 13, 2017, https://www.pewresearch.org/short-reads/2017/01/31/worlds-muslim-population-more-widespread-than-you-might-think/.

7. PEOPLE, IMMIGRANTS, AND REFUGEES

1. "Global Trends in Forced Displacement – 2020," UN Refugee Agency, June 17, 2022, https://www.unhcr.org/60b638e37/unhcr-global-trends-2020.
2. "Global Trends in Forced Displacement – 2020."
3. "Global Trends in Forced Displacement – 2020."
4. Edith M. Lederer, "Europe Accused of 'Double Standard' on Ukrainian Refugees," *AP News*, May 17, 2022, https://apnews.com/article/russia-ukraine-africa-government-and-politics-migration-09bd8954 82aa98a58d48e94630df9603.
5. Kyilah Terry, "The EU-Turkey Deal, Five Years On: A Frayed and Controversial but Enduring Blueprint," Migration Policy Institute, April 8, 2021, https://www.migrationpolicy.org/article/eu-turkey-deal-five-years-on.
6. Andrew Geddes, "The Politics of European Union Migration Governance," *Journal of Common Market Studies* 56, no. S1 (2018): 120–30.
7. Jon Erik Dølvik and Johannes Oldervoll, "Norway: Averting Crisis Through Coordination and Keynesian Welfare Policies," in *Welfare*

and the Great Recession: A Comparative Study, ed. Stefán Ólafsson et al. (Oxford: Oxford University Press, 2019), 210–27.

8. Mathew J. Creighton and Zan Strabac, "Party Affiliation and Support for Muslim Newcomers: Masked Opposition in the Norwegian Context," *European Societies* 22, no. 4 (2020): 480–502.

9. Creighton and Strabac, "Party Affiliation and Support."

10. Conrad Hacket et al., *The Global Religious Landscape: A Report on the Size and Distribution of the World's Major Religious Groups as of 2010* (Washington, DC: Pew Research Center, 2012).

CONCLUSION: MULTIPLE LAYERS, LEGAL REMEDIES, ANONYMOUS ACTS

1. Article 20 is divided into two parts. The first refers to war propaganda, but the second asks ratifying states to prohibit "any advocacy of national, racial or religious hatred that constitutes incitement to discrimination, hostility or violence." International Covenant on Civil and Political Rights, December 16, 1966, 999 U.N.T.S. 171, https://www.ohchr.org/en/instruments-mechanisms/instruments/international-covenant-civil-and-political-rights.

2. J. Glimerveen and J. Hagenbeek v/the Netherlands, Application Nos. 8348/78 and 8406/78, Decision of 11 October 1979 on the Admissibility of the Applications, https://hudoc.echr.coe.int/app/conversion/pdf/?library=ECHR&id=001-74187&filename=GLIMMERVEEN%20and%20HAGENBEEK%20v.%20othe%20NETHERLANDS.pdf.

3. *Legislating for Hate Speech and Hate Crime in Ireland: Report on the Public Consultation 2020* (Dublin: Department of Justice, 2020), https://assets.gov.ie/237922/07cb2005-2712-4808-9b48-348f224806b5.pdf.

4. Prohibition of Incitement to Hatred Act, 1989, November 29, 1989, https://www.irishstatutebook.ie/eli/1989/act/19/enacted/en/html.

5. Conor Gallagher, "Ireland First: Inside the Group Chat of Ireland's Latest Far-Right Political Party," *Irish Times*, March 12, 2023, https://www.irishtimes.com/ireland/social-affairs/2023/03/12/ireland-first-becomes-a-political-party-but-will-anyone-vote-for-it/.

6. Icek Ajzen and Martin Fishbein, "Attitude-Behavior Relations: A Theoretical Analysis and Review of Empirical Research," *Psychological Bulletin*

84, no. 5 (1977): 888; Icek Ajzen, "From Intentions to Actions: A Theory of Planned Behavior," in *Action Control: From Cognition to Behavior*, ed. Julius Kuhl and Jürgen Beckmann (Berlin: Springer, 1985), 11–39.

7. Icek Ajzen et al., "The Influence of Attitudes on Behavior," in *The Handbook of Attitudes*, 2nd ed., ed. Dolores Albarracin and Blair T. Johnson, vol. 1, *Basic Principles* (London: Routledge, 2018), 197–255.

8. David Neumark, "Detecting Discrimination in Audit and Correspondence Studies," *Journal of Human Resources* 47, no. 4 (2012): 1128–57.

9. Frank Dobbin, Daniel Schrage, and Alexandra Kalev, "Rage Against the Iron Cage: The Varied Effects of Bureaucratic Personnel Reforms on Diversity," *American Sociological Review* 80, no. 5 (2015): 1014–44.

10. Imogen Tyler and Tom Slater, "Rethinking the Sociology of Stigma," *Sociological Review* 66, no. 4 (2018): 721–43.

APPENDIX 1. CHAPTER 3 SURVEY EXPERIMENT: THE UNITED STATES BEFORE AND AFTER THE FINANCIAL CRISIS

1. Alexander Janus, "The List Experiment as an Unobtrusive Measure of Attitudes Toward Immigration and Same-Sex Marriages," Time-Sharing Experiments for the Social Sciences, 2005, https://www.tessexperiments.org/study/janus297.

2. Alexander L. Janus, "The Influence of Social Desirability Pressures on Expressed Immigration Attitudes," *Social Science Quarterly* 91, no. 4 (2010): 928–46.

3. Mathew J. Creighton and Amaney A. Jamal, "Perceptions of Islam, Migration and Citizenship in the United States: A List Experiment," Time-Sharing Experiments for the Social Sciences, 2010, https://www.tessexperiments.org/study/creighton022.

4. Mathew J. Creighton, Amaney Jamal, and Natalia C. Malancu, "Has Opposition to Immigration Increased in the United States After the Economic Crisis? An Experimental Approach," *International Migration Review* 49, no. 3 (2015): 727–56.

5. Creighton, Jamal, and Malancu, "Has Opposition to Immigration Increased."

6. E.g., Mathew J. Creighton et al., "Application of a List Experiment at the Population Level: The Case of Opposition to Immigration in the

Netherlands," in *Experimental Methods in Survey Research: Techniques That Combine Random Sampling with Random Assignment*, ed. Paul J. Lavrakas et al. (Hoboken, NJ: Wiley, 2019), 181–93.

APPENDIX 2. CHAPTERS 4 AND 6
SURVEY EXPERIMENTS: THE UNITED
KINGDOM BEFORE AND AFTER
THE BREXIT REFERENDUM

1. Mathew J. Creighton and Amaney A. Jamal, "An Overstated Welcome: Brexit and Intentionally Masked Anti-immigrant Sentiment in the UK," *Journal of Ethnic and Migration Studies* 48, no. 5 (2022): 1051–71.

APPENDIX 3. CHAPTER 5
SURVEY EXPERIMENTS: RACE
AND ETHNICITY IN IRELAND AND
THE NETHERLANDS

1. To learn more about the Economic and Social Research Institute, visit https://www.esri.ie/.
2. Information about the Labour Force Survey can be obtained from https://www.cso.ie/en/statistics/labourmarket/labourforcesurveylfs/.
3. Frances McGinnity, Mathew Creighton, and Éamonn Fahey, *Hidden Versus Revealed Attitudes: A List Experiment on Support for Minorities in Ireland* (Dublin: Economic and Social Research Institute, Irish Human Rights and Equality Commission, 2020); Mathew J. Creighton, Éamonn Fahey, and Frances McGinnity, "Immigration, Identity, and Anonymity: Intentionally Masked Intolerance in Ireland," *International Migration Review* 56, no. 3 (2022): 881–910.
4. For information on the LISS panel, visit https://www.lissdata.nl/.
5. The LISS panel data archive can be accessed at https://www.dataarchive.lissdata.nl/.
6. Mathew J. Creighton, Peter Schmidt, and Diana Zavala-Rojas, "Race, Wealth and the Masking of Opposition to Immigrants in the Netherlands," *International Migration* 57, no. 1 (2019): 245–63; Mathew J.

Creighton et al., "Application of a List Experiment at the Population Level: The Case of Opposition to Immigration in the Netherlands," in *Experimental Methods in Survey Research: Techniques That Combine Random Sampling with Random Assignment*, ed. Paul J. Lavrakas et al. (Hoboken, NJ: Wiley, 2019), 181–93.

APPENDIX 4. CHAPTER 6 SURVEY EXPERIMENTS: MUSLIM MIGRANTS IN THE UNITED STATES, IRELAND, AND THE NETHERLANDS

1. Mathew J. Creighton and Amaney Jamal, "Does Islam Play a Role in Anti-immigrant Sentiment? An Experimental Approach," *Social Science Research* 53 (2015): 89–103.

2. Mathew J. Creighton and Amaney A. Jamal, "Perceptions of Islam, Migration and Citizenship in the United States: A List Experiment," Time-Sharing Experiments for the Social Sciences, 2010, https://www .tessexperiments.org/study/creighton022.

3. To learn more about the Economic and Social Research Institute, visit https://www.esri.ie/.

4. Information about the Labour Force Survey can be obtained from https://www.cso.ie/en/statistics/labourmarket/labourforcesurveylfs/.

5. Frances McGinnity, Mathew Creighton, and Éamonn Fahey, *Hidden Versus Revealed Attitudes: A List Experiment on Support for Minorities in Ireland* (Dublin: Economic and Social Research Institute, Irish Human Rights and Equality Commission, 2020); Mathew J. Creighton, Éamonn Fahey, and Frances McGinnity, "Immigration, Identity, and Anonymity: Intentionally Masked Intolerance in Ireland," *International Migration Review* 56, no. 3 (2022): 881–910.

6. For information on the LISS panel, visit https://www.lissdata.nl/.

7. The LISS panel data archive can be accessed at https://www.dataarchive .lissdata.nl/.

8. Mathew J. Creighton, "Stigma and the Meaning of Social Desirability: Concealed Islamophobia in the Netherlands," in *Understanding Survey Methodology: Sociological Theory and Applications*, ed. Philip S. Brenner (Cham: Springer, 2020), 115–42.

APPENDIX 5. CHAPTER 7 SURVEY EXPERIMENT: PEOPLE, IMMIGRANTS, AND REFUGEES IN NORWAY

1. To learn more about the Norwegian Citizen Panel, visit https://www.uib.no/en/citizen/43063/about-panel.

2. Mathew J. Creighton and Zan Strabac, "Party Affiliation and Support for Muslim Newcomers: Masked Opposition in the Norwegian Context," *European Societies* 22, no. 4 (2020): 480–502.

INDEX

Page numbers in *italics* indicate figures or tables.

Printed and bound by CPI Group (UK) Ltd, Croydon, CR0 4YY

28/05/2024

14507718-0001